中国思想文化术语多语种对外翻译
标准化建设项目成果
CHINESE THINKING AND CULTURE
MULTILINGUAL TERMINOLOGY DATABASE

中华源·河南故事
CHINESE CIVILIZATION
Stories from Henan

中原粮谷
GRAIN OF CENTRAL PLAINS

河南省人民政府外事办公室　编

·郑州·

图书在版编目（CIP）数据

中华源·河南故事. 中原粮谷：汉英对照 / 河南省人民政府外事办公室编. -- 郑州：河南大学出版社，2022.8

ISBN 978-7-5649-5309-6

Ⅰ. ①中… Ⅱ. ①河… Ⅲ. ①地方文化－河南－通俗读物－汉、英②粮食－生产－河南－通俗读物－汉、英 Ⅳ. ①G127.61-49②F326.11-49

中国版本图书馆CIP数据核字（2022）第161669号

中原粮谷
ZHONGYUAN LIANGGU

责任编辑	卢志宇
责任校对	时　海
封面设计	翟淼淼
版式设计	李雪艳
出版发行	河南大学出版社
	地址：郑州市郑东新区商务外环中华大厦2401号　邮编：450046
	电话：0371-86059701（营销部）
	0371-86059750（高等教育与职业教育分公司）
	网址：hupress.henu.edu.cn
排　　版	河南大学出版社设计排版部
印　　刷	河南博雅彩印有限公司
版　　次	2022年8月第1版　　　印　次　2022年8月第1次印刷
开　　本	710 mm×1010 mm　1/16　　印　张　11.25
字　　数	189千字　　　　　　　　　定　价　57.00元

版权所有，侵权必究

本书如有印装质量问题，请与河南大学出版社营销部联系调换。

"中华源·河南故事"系列丛书编委会

顾　　问	黄友义	杨　平	范大祺			
主　　任	梁杰一					
副 主 任	卞　科	陈　岩	陈志伟	刁玉华	方启雄	韩国河
	惠　康	焦开举	介晓磊	孔留安	李冰冰	李　俊
	刘炯天	李向前	李　镇	梁留科	刘金锋	马萧林
	牛书成	牛卫国	屈凌波	屈鹏飞	史永庆	田　凯
	万正峰	王建修	王清义	王自文	许二平	杨建伟
	杨玮斌	俞海洛	张改平	张俊峰	张明超	张松文
	赵卫东					

主　　编	梁杰一					
副 主 编	李冰冰					
编　　委	陈国良	陈　玮	丁　锐	高　阳	徐恒振	郑延保
	孙立英	郭　远				

中华源·河南故事·中原粮谷

主　　编	卞　科
副 主 编	师高民　焦丹（英文）
中文撰稿	师高民
英文译者	焦　丹　张　翼　张桂芝
英文审校	[英国] Samuel Howarth
插　　图	谷创业　师晴怡　赵　星

The Editorial Committee
Chinese Civilization
Stories from Henan

Consultants	Huang Youyi Yang Ping Fan Daqi
Director	Liang Jieyi
Deputy Directors	Bian Ke Chen Yan Chen Zhiwei Diao Yuhua
	Fang Qixiong Han Guohe Hui Kang Jiao Kaiju
	Jie Xiaolei Kong Liu'an Li Bingbing Li Jun
	Liu Jiongtian Li Xiangqian Li Zhen Liang Liuke
	Liu Jinfeng Ma Xiaolin Niu Shucheng Niu Weiguo
	Qu Lingbo Qu Pengfei Shi Yongqing Tian Kai
	Wan Zhengfeng Wang Jianxiu Wang Qingyi Wang Ziwen
	Xu Erping Yang Jianwei Yang Weibin Yu Hailuo
	Zhang Gaiping Zhang Junfeng Zhang Mingchao
	Zhang Songwen Zhao Weidong
Chief Editor	Liang Jieyi
Deputy Chief Editor	Li Bingbing
Editors	Chen Guoliang Chen Wei Ding Rui Gao Yang
	Xu Hengzhen Zheng Yanbao Sun Liying Guo Yuan

Chinese Civilization
Stories from Henan
Grain of the Central Plains

Editor-in-Chief	Bian Ke
Associate Editors-in-Chief	Shi Gaomin
	Jiao Dan (English Text)
Writers	Shi Gaomin
Translators	Jiao Dan Zhang Yi Zhang Guizhi
Translation Proofreader	Samuel Howarth (UK)
Illustration	Gu Chuangye Shi Qingyi Zhao Xing

总　序

中国是世界四大文明古国之一，也是世界上唯一的古代文明传统未曾中断的国家。河南省地处中国中东部，是中华文明和中华民族的重要发祥地，在中国五千年的文明史上，河南作为国家政治、经济、文化的中心就长达三千多年。从某种意义上讲，一部河南史就是半部中国史。这里是中华人文始祖黄帝的故乡，是古丝绸之路的东方起点，是少林功夫和陈氏太极的发源地，这里创建了中国历史上最早的都城，镌刻了中国最古老的文字，诞生了中国最初的商业文明。

伴随着新时代的荣光，河南经济社会发展迅速，人民生活水平显著提升，这是河南人民自力更生、艰苦奋斗的历史结果，也是对外开放带来的益处。河南经济社会的发展、人民生活方式的改变都植根于深层次的文化积淀。为了让世界更多地了解河南，让河南更好地走向世界，2018年以来，河南省人民政府外事办公室认真研析了这片古老土地上的历史文化资源和时代风貌，组织各领域权威专家学者，编译了"中华源·河南故事"中外文系列丛书，选取黄河文化、河洛文化、老子、庄子、黄帝、少林功夫、太极拳、中医、汉字、丝绸之路、古都、农业、大运河、文物、陶瓷、青铜器、手工艺、书法、杂技、豫菜、豫剧、脱贫攻坚、空中丝绸之路、航空城、南水北调、中原粮谷、红旗渠、焦裕禄等多个主题，力图以故事的方式向世界展现一个立体、全面、真实的河南。

当今世界，人类文明无论是在物质还是在精神方面都取得了巨大进步，特别是物质的极大丰富，这在古代世界是完全不能想象的。同时，当代人类也面临着许多突出的难题，比如，贫富差距持续扩大，物欲追求奢华无度，个人主义恶性膨胀，社会诚信不断消减，伦理道德每况愈下，人与自然关系日趋紧张，等等。要解决这些难题，不仅需要运用人类今天的智慧和力量，而且需要运用人类历史上积累和储存的智慧和力量。河南历史文化底蕴深厚、包容性强，在今天仍极具现实意义。中原文化蕴含的思想智慧有助于修身养性，推动人类社会进步发展，焦裕禄精神、红旗渠精神所体现的为民爱民、艰苦奋斗的价值取向是构建人类命运共同体的力量源泉。我们期待与读者们一起从河南故事中汲取更多的智慧和力量，共同创造更加美好的未来。

Series Foreword

China is one of the four ancient civilizations in the world, and is also the only country in the world where the ancient civilization has not been interrupted. Located in east-central China, Henan Province is an important cradle for the Chinese nation and Chinese civilization. In the course of the five thousand years of Chinese history, for more than three thousand years it served as the political, economic and cultural center of the country and therefore, as generally accepted, represents half of the history of China. Henan is the native place of Yellow Emperor, the cradle of Chinese culture, the starting point of the ancient Silk Road in the east, and the birthplace of Shaolin Kungfu and Chen-style Taijiquan—typical examples of the world-renowned Chinese martial arts. It was here that the earliest capital city in China was founded, the oldest Chinese characters engraved, and the earliest commerce took shape.

In the new era, Henan has witnessed rapid growth in its economy and remarkable improvement of people's living conditions owing to the national reform and opening-up policy and unremitting endeavors of the people. Modern economic achievements and social development as well as the changes of way of life could be traced back to its traditional values and cultural heritages. To enable people from other countries to understand Henan, and let the Province integrate more efficiently into the world development, the Foreign Affairs Office of the People's Government of Henan Province has organized teams of authoritative experts and scholars in relevant fields to compile this *Chinese Civilization: Stories from Henan* in Chinese and foreign languages since 2018 by crystallizing the excellence of traditions and outstanding features of modern development. The book series include *The Yellow River Culture*, *Heluo Culture*, *Laozi*, *Zhuangzi*, *The Yellow Emperor*, *Shaolin Kungfu*, *Taijiquan*, *Traditional Chinese Medicine*,

Chinese Characters, The Silk Road, Ancient Chinese Capitals, Feeding the People—Agriculture, The Grand Canal, Cultural Heritage, Ceramic, Bronze, Handicraft Art, Calligraphy, Acrobatics, Henan Cuisine, Henan Opera, Poverty Alleviation, Silk Road in the Air, Zhengzhou—An Aviation City, South-to-North Water Diversion, Grain of the Central Plains, Man-Made River—Hongqiqu Canal, A Model Official—Jiao Yulu, etc., presenting a panoramic picture of the Province.

In today's world, human civilization has made great progress in both material accumulation and ethical advancement, and the great abundance of materials today, especially, is beyond the imagination of the ancient people. At the same time, however, modern people are also confronted with a lot of problems, such as the widening gap between the rich and the poor, the indulgence in pursuit of luxury and extravagance, the undesirable extension of individualism, the decline of social integrity, and the increasingly tense relationship between man and nature. To solve the problems, we need to draw on the wisdom and powers developed today as well as those accumulated in the past. Henan is endowed with rich historical and cultural heritages characterized by its inclusiveness, and such heritages remain significant today. The intelligence and wisdom in Henan culture are conducive to self-cultivation and to the promotion of social development. The spirit of serving the people and relentless struggle, as embodied in Jiao Yulu and the man-made river—Hongqiqu Canal provides source of strength for building a community with a shared future for mankind. It is our hope that wisdom and strength from Henan stories could lead us to a shared brilliant future.

前　言

中华民族在几千年的农耕文明进程中，笃志跋拓，奉行民以食为天的崇高理念，辛勤耕耘，力田为生，祈望风调雨顺，粮丰廪实，向往山河无恙，岁月静好。从秦汉帝国奠定的农业定居区起，在漫长坎坷的时代变迁中，壮美悠久的大河南就稳居九州之中，充当着撼天动地、无与伦比的重要角色。

中原厚土，豫地胜壤，这一片神奇的土地，山川形胜，阡陌纵横，沃野千里，在中国历代的八大古都中独占四席。行之所至，处处都散落着粮食文化的宝贵遗产；目之所及，处处都刻录着文明进步的时代履痕。大河之南的一方热土，充满着历史的魅力，跃动着发展的活力，蕴含着文化的张力，其独特的地域个性、鲜活的人文情貌、绵长的历史记载，恰如温润的中华襁褓，忠实地展示了中华民族成形、成长、成熟、成功、成就的漫长历程，叙说了几千年来从未中断、流传有序的华夏文明，谱写着栉风沐雨中淬砺奋发的光辉篇章。

博大精深的粮食文化勾画了社会前进的宏大风景。从古老原始的自然经济状态到现代化的"粮食产储运加贸一体化全流程"的完整产业链条，中国的粮食产业经历了无数次的鱼龙蜕变和华美转身。勤劳朴实的中原儿女在历史的大变革中始终秉持天道酬勤的优良传统，专注埋头干，鲜刷存在感，以大豫精神塑造大音稀声、大象无形、大器晚成的大省形象，筚路蓝缕，披荆斩棘，不断迈向辉煌的境界。

河南，是中国之中原之地，素有豫州、中州之称。河南粮食产量一直超中国总产量的十分之一，小麦产量稳居中国之首，粮食转化加工位居中国第一，中国市场上 1/3 的方便面、1/4 的馒头、3/5 的汤圆、7/10 的水饺产自河南，在粮食领域牢牢占据执牛耳、牵龙头、摘桂冠之大位，人口大省的河南由此成为实至名归的粮食大省。河南粮食及粮制品的丰歉盈缺、产储运加直接关联着中国粮食的供需平衡，影响着中国经济社会发展的大局，有牵发动身、举足轻重之地位。由低到高、由弱到强、由粗到精、由分到合，河南粮食产业在历经艰辛开拓、浴火淬炼的嬗变后，终于从"大粮仓"进入"大厨房"，登上"大餐桌"，个中情由，悉发自深厚的历史渊源。

粮食乃国家之重，安全乃粮食之重。仓廪实，天下安。星罗棋布坐落在中原大地上的古代大粮仓，设计精巧，规模宏大，声名远播，令人震撼。浚县的黎阳仓，巩义的洛口仓，洛阳的回洛仓、含嘉仓等，这些镶嵌在广阔田畴上的人文瑰宝，无可置疑地成为河南人为之荣耀的鸿篇巨制。贯通于公元 7 世纪的隋唐大运河，也曾经千舟竞发，川流不息，成为沟通南北、推动粮食流通贸易的时代杰作，为历代王朝的文功武治、政权巩固发挥了重要作用。仓储与漕运结合，历史上数度创造了民殷国富、繁荣太平的盛世风光，为统治阶级安邦治国提供了最重要的物质保障。18 世纪法国哲学家孟德斯鸠曾言，小国灭于外敌，大国亡于内乱。帝国王朝正由于手中有粮，才能一次次地避免和消解黎庶涂炭、乾坤倾覆的危局，在风雨飘摇中，一次次反转粮匮民乱的剧情，治乱抚民，实现四海安澜、五业发达的和平愿景。

几千年农耕文明陶冶的乡土中国，从农耕、保守、封闭、礼治的传统形态，在长期艰难的嬗变中，化茧成蝶，转换到工商、进取、开放、法治的现代轨道。

经过长期努力，中国特色社会主义进入新时期，这是中国发展新的历史方位。为全面贯彻"一带一路""人类命运共同体"倡议，落实"中国人要把饭碗端在自己手里，而且要装自己的粮食；悠悠万事，吃饭为大"的指示精神，在保证粮食稳定增产基础上，推动产后各环节以至消费终端，同时发力，齐头并进，壮大粮食经济，中国各地涌现了一批在粮食储运、贸易、科技创新等方面的上乘之作。河南在国家政策支持下，顺风借力，当行出色，在扩大粮食产能、优化专业教育、提升科技水平、保证交易质量等方面，瞄准发展目标，拓宽发展空间，以大力度营造粮食大格局，促推粮食食品加工和深加工，不断延伸粮食食品产业链，提高经济效益，保证社会效益，在中国乃至全球独树一帜。

粮食给人以生存的营养和能量，平凡的土地给珍贵的粮食以滋养和基础。当前，正值百年未有之大变局，在新形势下，面临新挑战、新机遇，中原粮食应贯彻落实"藏粮于地""藏粮于技"，强基固本，确保国家粮食安全，努力收获新成果，不断迈上新台阶，为造福民生、壮大国力继续做出新的贡献。

河南是中国粮谷的一面旗帜，为泱泱大中华悠悠五千年的时和世泰及福寿康宁奠定坚实基础，筑牢安全城墙。

中原大粮仓，国脉永担当。

千年主沉浮，古今竞辉煌。

Preface

Over the thousands of years of farming civilization, the Chinese nation has devoted itself to the noble idea that grain is the first necessity of the people. The Chinese nation has worked arduously to make a living from the farms, praying for good weather and abundant grain, yearning for safe living, and peaceful years. Since the agricultural settlements in the Qin and Han empires, throughout the long and rolling waves of the times, Henan, with its magnificent and long-standing history in China, has played an unparalleled and crucial role.

Rich in soil and endowed with great mountains and rivers, crisscross paths and fertile fields, the magical land of Henan used to be home to four of China's eight ancient capitals. The precious heritage of grain culture and the traces of civilization's progress are recorded everywhere. The promising land in the south of the Yellow River is charming with its rich history, vigorous progress and cultural force. Its unique topography, vivid humanistic spirit and long historical records, the geographical and cultural swaddling of mother China, faithfully demonstrate the Chinese nation's long process of the formation, growth, maturity, success and achievements. The land of Henan consistently narrates thousands of years of Chinese civilization and composes a glorious chapter of arduous efforts in spite of the wind and the rain.

The extensive and profound culture of grain has painted the grand landscape society's development. From the natural economy in ancient times to the complete industrial chain of "the whole integration process of the grain production, storage, transportation, processing and trade" in modern times, China's grain industry has undergone numerous and marvelous transformations. Throughout the great changes of history, adhering to the law of "God rewards the diligent", and imbued with the Henan spirit, the industrious and modest people of the Central Plains devoted themselves to hard work, and forged the mythos of a quiet powerful province, the imperceptible later bloomer. They restlessly strove to create an illustrious kingdom.

Henan, the Central Plains of China, is also named as Yuzhou and Zhongzhou. Henan's total grain output has always exceeded one tenth of China's annual grain output. Henan's wheat production and grain conversion processing are the best in China. In the Chinese market, one third of instant noodles, one fourth of steamed buns, three fifths of glutinous rice dumplings, and seven tenth dumplings are produced in Henan. It is clear to see that Henan is the king of grain. Henan has grown from a province with a large population into a province with a vast grain output. The balance of supply and demand of grain in China is directly affected by the production, storage and transportation of the grain and its products in Henan, and so Henan plays an influential role in China's overall economic and social development. Over the course of its long-term development from the low to high, weak to strong, coarse to fine, divided to collected, Henan's grain industry has undergone a transformation from being known as "the big barn" to "the big kitchen" on the grain output of which is served on "the big table".

Grain is the nation's most important provision, and grain security is essential. Sufficient grain guarantees the nation's security. The grant ancient granaries which were exquisitely designed and widely scattered on the land of the Central Plains are particularly amazing. Liyang Granary in Xunxian County, Luokou Granary in Gongxian County, Huiluo Granary and Hanjia Granary in Luoyang, are regarded as cultural treasures embedded in vast fields and as the glorious masterpieces of Henan people. The Grand Canal in the Sui and Tang dynasties, which ran through the seventh century AD, also is a real masterpiece in that it linked up the north and the south of the country, continues promoting grain circulation and trade, and playing an important role in the civil and military governance as well as the consolidation of political stability for successive dynasties. For several dynasties, the people and the country prospered thanks to the combination of warehousing and water transport, which provided the most fundamental material guarantee for the authority of the ruling class. Montesquieu, an 18th century French philosopher, once remarked that small countries are destroyed by foreign enemies while big countries are destroyed by civil strife. Grain enabled the imperial dynasty to avoid the danger of the common people being repeatedly plunged into misery and chaos. Despite the wind and rain, it is also the grain that helped the imperial court to weather chaotic periods of history chaotic times and ensure a peaceful life for China's people.

With its thousands of years of agricultural civilization, China has transitioned from the traditional mode of farming, conservation, closed and ritual governance, to the modern path of industry and commerce, progression, openness, and the rule of law.

After determined, China with socialist characteristics has entered a new era that reflects a new historical orientation for its development. In order to fully implement the initiative of "Belt and Road""A Community of Shared Future for Mankind" and the calls for Chinese people of "taking the matter of grain security firmly into own hands", on the basis of the steady increase of grain production, China should work hard on promoting all aspects of post-production and consumption terminals to boost the grain economy. A number of fruitful achievements in grain storage and transportation, trade, scientific and technological innovation have taken place across China. With the support of national policy, Henan has made great efforts to expand grain production capacity, optimize professional education, upgrade the level of science and technology, and ensure the quality of transactions. Henan aims to fulfill development goals and broaden development potentials, so as to plot the course for grain, promote the grain processing and deep processing, and continuously extend the grain industry chain. The level of importance which China attaches to the development of its grain industry is rarely seen in other parts of the world.

Grain provides people with nutrition and the energy to survive, while the land nourishes and lays the foundation for grain. Under the current global situation and as we face new challenges and opportunities, the grain industry of the Central Plains will demonstrate the plan to "store grain on soil" and "store grain in technology", so as to strengthen the foundation to ensure national grain security, strive to create new achievements, and continue to reach a new level and do what we can to the benefit of people's livelihood and national strength.

Henan is seen as the standard-bearer for China's grain, laying a solid foundation and safeguarding China's development and prosperity for over the five thousand years.

The granary of the Central Plains bears the lifeblood of the nation.

Thousands of years of rains and storms are the granary's brilliant and precious charm.

目 录   Contents

第一章　廪实仓盈　001
- 一、粮食储藏探源　002
- 二、仓储设施种类　010
- 三、粮食储藏史说　016
- 四、社会公益储备　026
- 五、政府粮食储备　038
- 六、历代著名粮仓　044

Chapter 1　Rich and Ample Granary Storage　001
- Ⅰ. The Roots of Grain Storage　003
- Ⅱ. Varieties of Grain Storage Facilities　011
- Ⅲ. The History of Grain Storage　017
- Ⅳ. Public Welfare Grain Reserve　027
- Ⅴ. Government Grain Reserve　039
- Ⅵ. Famous Granaries through the Ages　045

第二章　谷脉流长　061
- 一、粮食贸易探源　062
- 二、粮食贸易属性　072
- 三、古代粮食运输　080

Chapter 2　History of Grain Circulation　061
- Ⅰ. The Origins of Grain Trade　063
- Ⅱ. The Nature of Grain Trade　073
- Ⅲ. Grain Transportation in Ancient Times　081

第三章　漕运春秋　089
- 一、跌宕兴衰　090

二、转漕、漕挈与中转粮仓　　098
　　三、漕运路道与运行　　110
　　四、"南粮北调"与"北粮南运"　　112

Chapter 3　History of Water Transportation　　089
　　Ⅰ. Rise and Decline　　091
　　Ⅱ. Land-to-water Transportation, Water-to-land Transportation and
　　　　Grain Transfer Granary　　099
　　Ⅲ. The Route and Operation of Water Transportation　　111
　　Ⅳ. The Grain Transfer of South-to-North and North-to-South　　113

第四章　中国粮策　　117
　　一、中国粮食安全特色之路　　118
　　二、中国粮食对外开放与国际合作　　126
　　三、中国粮食未来展望与政策主张　　128
　　四、现代粮食科技创新——中国粮谷　　134

Chapter 4　China's Grain Policy　　117
　　I. Grain Security in China　　119
　　II. Opening Up and International Cooperation of China's Grain　　127
　　III. Prospects and Policies of China's Grain　　129
　　IV. Modern Grain Scientific Technology Innovation—China's
　　　　Grain Valley　　135

第五章　中原粮谷　　143
　　一、最高粮食学府——郑州粮食学院　　146
　　二、首个粮食史馆——中国粮食博物馆　　148

三、首部粮食史书——《中国粮食史图说》　　152

Chapter 5　Achievements of the Central Plains' Grain　　143
　　I. Zhengzhou Grain College — the Supreme Grain Institution of China　　147
　　II. China Grain Museum — the First Grain History Museum　　149
　　III. *Chinese Grain History with Illustrations* — The First Historical Book on China's Grain　　153

参考文献　　156
References　　157

后　记　　158
Postscript　　159

附录：中国历史年代简表　　160
Appendix: A Brief Chronology of Chinese History　　160

第一章

廪实仓盈

Chapter 1

Rich and Ample Granary Storage

古语说："兵马未动，粮草先行。"粮食储藏是粮食生产的继续，发明创造粮食储藏方法特别重要且意义深远。科学的粮食储藏措施可减少粮食损失，增加贮备，抵御灾害，强国富民。

一、粮食储藏探源

中国的粮食储藏起源很早。先民们在收集野生粮食之时，会将一时食用不完的粮食储藏起来，这就是粮食储藏的起源，约始见于农业生产粮食之前，出现于新石器时代之初。当时，已经有瓮、罐之类可以用于储藏。

到了文字出现时，粮食储藏开始见于古文献记载，根据文字记录，可以证明粮食储藏的历史情况。

灰陶印纹卧鼻罐·未来古代粮食文化陈列馆藏
Grey Clay Plating Can of Lying Nose-shape ·
Collected by Future Ancient Grain Culture Exhibition Hall

As the old saying goes, "Before dispatching soldiers and horses, take care of the grain",which is reflecting the crucial importance of grain in times of war. Grain storage is the continuation of grain production, and so invention of grain storage technologies is particularly important and of far-reaching significance. Grain storage technologies can reduce grain loss, increase storage volume, resist disasters, strengthen the country and enrich the people.

I. The Roots of Grain Storage

First appearing at the dawn of the Neolithic Age, China's first attempts at grain storage took place quite early in the nation's history. When our ancestors collected wild food, surpluses were stored, and this was the origin of grain storage. At that time, urns and pots were already being used for storage.

Afterwards, the invention of Chinese characters made it possible for grain storage recorded in ancient literature, and so we have supporting evidence for the historical development of grain storage.

红陶瓮（屈家岭文化）· 湖南省博物馆藏
Red Pottery Urn (Qujialing Culture) · Collected by Hunan Provincial Museum

1. Exploration of Ancient Literature

In the pre-Qin period of China, *The Book of Songs* and *The Rites of Zhou*

红陶罐（仰韶文化）·中国粮食博物馆藏
Red Pottery Pot (Yangshao Culture) · Collected by Chinese Grain Museum

1. 古文献探源

在中国先秦时期，《诗经》和《周礼》是两部特别珍贵的典籍，其内容真实可信。在这两部著作中，记载了数种应用于粮食储藏的设施。

《诗经·小雅·甫田》："曾孙之庾，如坻如京。乃求千斯仓，乃求万斯箱。黍稷稻粱，农夫之庆。报以介福。"

《诗经·小雅·楚茨》："我稷翼翼。我仓既盈，我庾维亿。"

《王祯农书》："庾者，露积谷也。仓，房屋者。我庾维亿，积谷多也。"又："京，仓之方者。"

以下是常见的粮食储藏设施与方法。

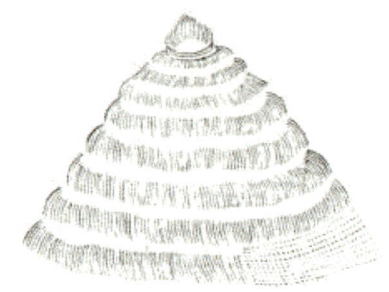

庾
Yu

represent two examples particularly precious and reliable classical literature in which several grain storages were recorded.

> *The Fields ·Psalms Minor · The Book of Songs*
> The grandson's bins o'erfill
> And stand there tall as the hill.
> Thousands of barns are built;
> Myriads carts are gilt.
> The grains are hauled and stored;
> And we rejoice with the Lord.
> The Lord's with fortune blessed.

> *Lush Thorns · Psalms Minor · The Book of Songs*
> My sorghum does excel.
> After a year of pains,
> My garner's full of grains.

> *The Agricultural Book of Wang Zhen* explains that "Yu" is an open granary, "Cang", a warehouse, and that "Jing" is a square warehouse.
> Zhen then tells that his "open granary is full of grain".

The following images depict commonly-used grain storage facilities and approaches.

> *Lord Liu · Psalms Major · The Book of Songs*
> He planned and tilled the fields
> And stored in barns the yields.
> Here and there the grain stacks,
> He filled all bags and all sacks.

廪
Lin

《诗·大雅·公刘》："乃场乃疆，乃积乃仓，乃裹糇粮。"又《诗·周颂·丰年》："丰年多黍多稌，亦有高廪，万亿及秭。"

《王祯农书》："廪，仓别名。廪所以藏粢盛之穗。今农家构为无壁厦屋，以贮禾穗及穜稑之种。"

《周礼·地官》（卷十六）："廪人，掌九谷之数，以待国之匪颁，周赐稍食。""仓人：掌粟入之藏，辨九谷之物，以待邦用。若谷不足，则止余法用，有余则藏之，以待凶而颁之。"汉郑玄注："九谷尽藏焉，以粟为主。"

《夏商周断代工程》有载，《诗经》和《周礼》中所记叙的内容，距今约有 3500 年的历史。由于粮食储藏设施的创造发明会远早于典籍记载，所以中国的粮食仓贮起源应当早于商周时期，即便从夏朝算起，至今也已有 4000 余年的历史。

2. 考古发现探源

在中国许多考古发现中，例如在陕西西安市半坡村、河北武安市磁山、河南新郑市裴李岗等地，都发现了新石器时代的粟，有的储藏于陶

Chapter 1 Rich and Ample Granary Storage Grain

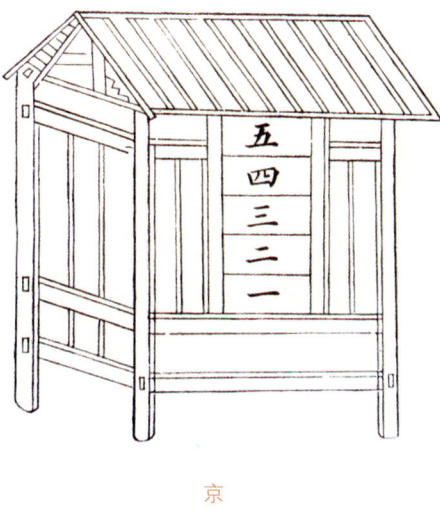

京
Jing

A Good Year · Chants of Chou · The Book of Songs
Much millet and rice in a good year,
High barns rush to appear,
A million front to rear.

According to *The Agricultural Book of Wang Zhen*: "Lin is another name for a warehouse, used to store food and the seeds of the grain."

Di Guan · The Volume 16 of *The Rites of Zhou* records: "Linren, the official in charge of the grain supply, prepares for the state to pay the ministers and for charitable grain to relieve the needy. Cangren is responsible for the grain storage. The cangren classifies the names and types of the grains for the use of the kingdom. Once grain is insufficient, the grain consumption is reduced; when surplus, it will be stored for use in famine years." Zheng Xuan, the scholar and master in the late Eastern Han dynasty, noted that, "The grain is full stored with millet as the main part."

Recorded in *The Xia-Shang-Zhou Chronology Project, The Book of Songs*

瓮或双耳陶罐中。经研究测定，这些珍藏着粮食的设施距今大约已有5000年至6000年的历史。

尖底罐·半坡村遗址
Bottom-pointed Bottle · The Banpo Village Site

红陶双耳三足壶（裴李岗文化）·中国粮食博物馆藏
Red Pottery of Two-ear and Three-legged Pot (Peiligang Culture) · Collected by Chinese Grain Museum

and *The Rites of Zhou* span a history of around 3,500 years. Since the creation and invention of grain storage facilities took place long before the earliest classical records, it is assumed that grain storage first began in China before the time of the Shang and Zhou dynasties. Even calculated from the Xia dynasty, grain storage still has a history of over 4,000 years.

2. Archaeological Discoveries

In many archaeological sites in China, such as the Banpo village in Xi'an city, Shaanxi province, the Cishan village in Wu'an city, Hebei province, and the Peiligang village in Xinzheng city, Henan province, Neolithic millet has been discovered in pottery urns and two-ear pottery cans. Studies determine that these grain storage facilities are around 5,000 to 6,000 years old.

Rice and other cereals from the Neolithic Age, stored in granary or pottery, have been discovered at archaeological sites such as Hemudu in Yuyao city, Zhejiang province, Pengtou Mountain in Lixian county, Hunan province, Qujialing in Jingshan county, Hubei province, Pao Maling in Xiushui county, Jiangxi province, Baiyang Village in Binchuan county, Yunnan province, Caoxie Mountain in Wujiang city, Jiangsu province and Songze of Qingpu district, Shanghai municipality. It has been determined that these grain storage facilities are approximately 5,000 to 6,000 years old.

灰陶彩绘龙纹陶仓（汉代）• 中国粮食博物馆藏
Grey Pottery Granary with Painted Dragon Pattern (Han dynasty) • Collected by Chinese Grain Museum

半坡村遗址
The Banpo Village Site

在浙江余姚市河姆渡、湖南澧县彭头山、湖北京山县屈家岭、江西修水县跑马岭、云南宾川县白羊村、江苏吴江市草鞋山、上海青浦崧泽等考古遗址中也都发现了新石器时代的稻谷及其他谷物，有的稻谷储藏在仓房里或陶器中。经研究测定，这些储藏着粮食的设施距今约有5000年至6000年的历史。

总之，许多考古发现表明，中国是世界上最早发明创造粮食储藏技术的国家之一，至今已有数千年历史，而且储藏技术高明，居世界领先地位。

二、仓储设施种类

中国古人发明的粮食储藏设施门类很多，科技原理精湛高超，造型丰富多样，外观优美，富有创意。根据古书上的论述及考古发现的实物，可将其进行分类。

彩绘龙纹陶仓（汉代）·中国粮食博物馆藏
Granary with Painted Dragon Pattern (Han dynasty) ·
Collected by Chinese Grain Museum

In short, many archaeological findings show that China is one of the first countries in the world that invent grain storage technology, with its history of several thousands of years, resulting in China's leading position in terms of brilliant storage technology.

II. Varieties of Grain Storage Facilities

Different varieties of grain storage facilities were invented by ancient Chinese people. The facilities made use of superb scientific and technological theories, diverse construction styles, exquisite in their appearance and the creativity. Thanks to the records contained in ancient texts we are able to classify grain storage technologies according to the table below.

1. 储藏设施分类

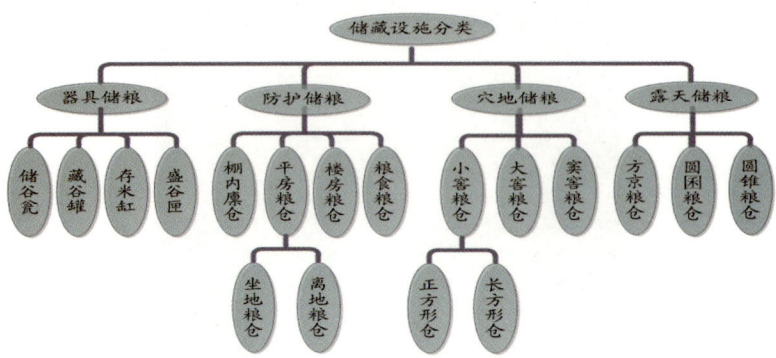

2. 古代储粮设施

储谷瓮·海南省博物馆藏
Grain Urn · Collected by Hainan Museum

藏谷罐·山东长江集团藏
Grain Jar · Collected by Shandong Changjiang Company

平房离地仓 · 银川省博物馆藏
Horizontal Warehouse off the Ground · Collected by the Yinchuan Museum

1. Classification of Storage Facilities

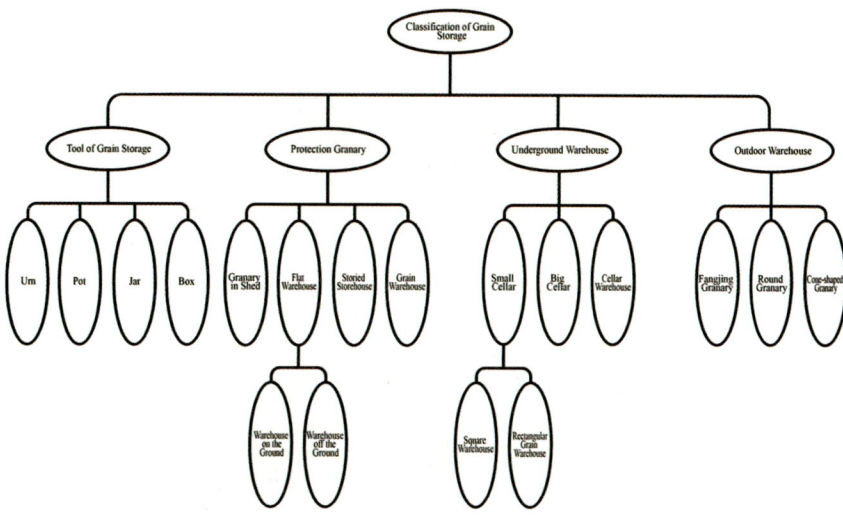

2. Ancient Storage Facilities

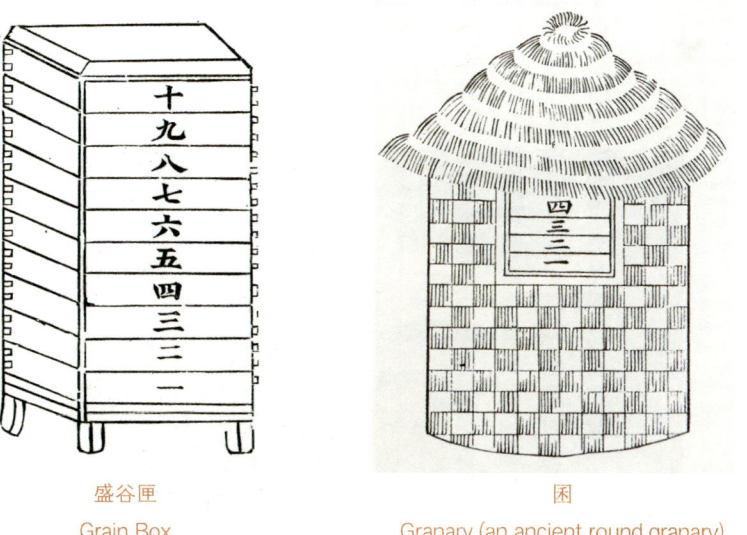

盛谷匣
Grain Box

困
Granary (an ancient round granary)

第一章　廪实仓盈

平房坐地仓
Horizontal Warehouse on the Ground

三筒楼仓・中国国家博物馆藏
Storied Triple Silo・Collected by National Museum of China

三层楼仓
Tri-storied Granary

离地陶仓
Pottery Barn off the Ground

囷　　　　　　　陶囷·中国粮食博物馆藏
Granary　　　Pottery Granary · Collected by Chinese Grain Museum

房形陶仓（汉）·中国粮食博物馆藏
House-shaped Pottery Barn（Han dynasty）· Collected by Chinese Grain Museum

异形陶仓 1
Special-shaped Pottery Barn 1

敖房仓
Aofang Barn

三、粮食储藏史说

中国粮食储藏建设起源于新石器时代,至今约有 5000 年至 6000 年历史。到了商周时期,民间大量储藏粮食,已较常见。如前面列举《诗经》中的"甫田""楚茨""丰田"等,所记叙的贮粮都是民间储藏法。《周

异形陶仓 2 · 中国粮食博物馆藏
Special-shaped Pottery Barn 2 · Collected by Chinese Grain Museum

异形陶仓 3 · 中国粮食博物馆藏
Special-shaped Pottery Barn 3 · Collected by Chinese Grain Museum

III. The History of Grain Storage

The grain storage in China originated in the Neolithic Age with a history of around 5,000 to 6,000 years. In the Shang and Zhou dynasties, it was common for people to store grain in large quantities. For example, the "Futian" "Chuci" "Fengtian" mentioned in *The Book of Songs* were the storage approaches of the common people. Records in *The Rites of Zhou* testify to the emergence of a state law for grain storage.

It is common knowledge that from the Shang and Zhou dynasties, China's fortune has always been inevitably determined by abundance or shortage in grain. Since grain production developed at the same time as construction of granaries, historical texts recorded the building of a variety of private granaries in addition to those operated by the state.

礼》中对贮粮的记载，是国家粮仓贮备法面世的证据。

自商周时代以来，举国上下已知，国家兴亡与粮食富足或短缺有关。粮食生产与粮仓建造同时发展，在史书上除了国家粮仓外，还有私人粮仓的记载。

1. 汉朝时期

首先是国家粮仓，规模很大，贮粮种类很多。粮食流通与分配、入仓与消费以及粮食管理等皆由国家专门机构负责。在古书上，国家粮仓出现于秦汉间，著名的有太仓和甘泉仓。

> 司马迁《史记·平准书》："汉兴七十余年间，国家无事……京师之钱累巨万，贯朽而不可校；太仓之粟陈陈相因，充溢露积于外，至腐败而不可食。"
>
> 司马迁《史记·平准书》："桑弘羊又请令民，得入粟补吏，及罪以赎。令民能入粟甘泉……诸农各致粟，山东漕益岁六百万石。一岁之中，太仓、甘泉仓满。"

根据研究，"太仓"在西汉京师长安，是国家大粮仓。"甘泉仓"在京师西北淳化县甘泉山中，距长安约二百里，山中有汉武帝的避暑行宫。

其次，国家首建"常平仓"，私人经营的"窖仓"买卖粮食已经出现。

> 《汉书·食货志》："宣帝（刘询）即位（公元前73年），用吏

1. The Han Dynasty

First, the national granary, built on large scale, is composed of variety of different types of grain storage. Grain circulation and distribution, warehousing and consumption, as well as grain management all fall under the responsibility of specialized state agencies. In ancient books, the famous Tai granary and Ganquan granary were built in the Qin and Han dynasties.

In his *Pingzhun Book·Records of the Grand Historian,* Sima Qian wrote: "So that it was peaceful for more than seventy years since the founding of the Han dynasty, thousands of coins were accumulated in the capital, and the string holding coins together would fray under the weight. The grain in Tai granary was piled up year after year over flowing, in the open air, rotten and inedible."

Sima Qian wrote that Sang Hongyang also suggested allowing petty officials be promoted on the basis of grain donation, and ordered the people to pay grain to Ganquan Palace. The agricultural officials from all over the country sent grain one after another, and the amount of grain transported from the east of Xiaoshan Mountain increased to six million *dan* a year. The Tai granary and Ganquan granary are full of grain within one year.

Research shows that Tai granary was a national granary in Chang'an, the capital of the Eastern Han dynasty. Ganquan granary was located in Ganquan Mountain, Chunhua County, around 200 miles northwest of Chang'an. On the mountain stood the summer palace of Emperor Wu of the Han dynasty.

Besides, the state built Changping granary, after the face of the privately-run grain trading Jiao granary.

It is written in *Food Commodities·The History of the Former Han Dynasty* that "after Emperor Xuan (Liu Xun) of the Han dynasty ascended the throne (73 BC), more virtuous officials were promoted to key positions. At that time, Geng Shouchang, an agricultural official, proposed to build granaries in the border areas and raise the price of

多选贤良……大司农中丞耿寿昌奏令边郡皆筑仓，以谷贱时增其价而籴以利农，谷贵时减价而粜，名曰常平仓。"

《史记·货殖列传》："宣曲任氏之先，为督道仓吏。秦之败也，豪杰皆争取金玉，而任氏独窖仓积粟。楚、汉相拒荥阳也，民不得耕种，米石至万，而豪杰金玉尽归任氏。任氏以此起富。"

2. 魏晋南北朝时期

魏武帝曹操，权势极大，迁献帝到河南许昌定都，自命丞相。他的帝称是由其儿子曹丕在称帝后追封的。自魏晋至南北朝时期起，国家破碎，长期战乱不断。特殊时代背景下所建造的粮仓，其性质和作用也很特殊。

晋武帝承前朝建常平仓。

《晋书·食货志》："武帝（司马炎）欲平一江表……乃立常平仓，丰则籴，俭则粜，以利百姓……敕戒郡国计吏，诸郡国守相、令长，务尽地利，禁游食商贩。"

grain in order to protect the interests of farmers when the market price was low; when the market price rose, it was sold at a reduced price. One such granary after this model is named Changping granary".

In *The Money-makers·Records of the Grand Historian,* it is claimed that "the ancestor of the Ren family of Xuanqu was a granary officer at Dudao. When the Qin Empire was overthrown and the better off citizens were scrambling for gold and jade, Ren's family were the only ones to store up grain. Soon the armies of Chu and Han were locked in battle at Xingyang. The peasants could not farm and the price of a picul of rice rose to ten thousand. Gold and jade flowed to the Rens, who made a fortune".

2. The Wei, Jin, Southern and Northern Dynasties

In China's long history, Cao Cao, Emperor Wu of the Wei dynasty, was extremely powerful. He held Emperor Xian under his influence and settled the capital in Xuchang, Henan Province, before appointing himself the prime minister. His imperial title was given by his son Cao Pi after Cao Pi proclaimed himself emperor. From the times of the Wei and Jin dynasties to the Northern and Southern dynasties, the country was fractured with constant and protracted wars. Built under such a unique historical period, these granaries were therefore very special in their nature and function.

Emperor Wu of the Jin dynasty inherited the Changping granary from his dynastic predecessors.

Food Commodities·Book of Jin has it that "the Emperor Wu (Sima Yan) intended to unify the regions south of the Yangtze River, and so he set up Changping granary. In the harvest years, grain was purchased and stored in large quantities at a low price, while in the famine years, the grain was sold in large quantities to stabilize prices to benefit farmers. He also ordered the county magistrates to increase the production of land as much as possible and prohibit the activities of vagrants and traders".

The establishment of such granaries can stabilize grain prices and crack down

这是建粮仓稳粮价打击投机商之策。

北魏孝文帝求安民术，建安民粮仓。

《魏书·食货志》："帝（孝文帝）十二年（公元 488 年），诏群臣求安民术。帝寻施行焉：各令官司，丰年籴贮于仓，时俭则加私之一，粜之于民。如此民必力田，积财以取粟。……一夫之田，岁积六十斛……数年之中则谷积民足矣。"

这是建粮仓安民求发展之策。

北魏庄帝颁纳粮赐官令，建粮仓。

《魏书·食货志》："庄帝初（公元 528 年），承丧乱之后，仓廪虚罄，遂班入粟之制。输粟八千石，赏散侯；六千石，散伯……职人输七百石，赏一大阶，授以实官……诸沙门有输粟四千石入京仓者，授本州统。"

on speculators.

The Emperor Xiaowen of the Northern Wei dynasty built granaries in a bid for harmony for his people.

Food Commodities·Book of Wei describes that "in the 12th year of the Emperor Xiaowen of the Northern Wei dynasty (488 AD), the emperor requested the ministers for practical advice in governance. Special organizations for administrative management were set up for the purpose of giving such advice. In the harvest years, the surplus grain was stored in the granary, while in the famine years, stored grain was sold to the people at a mark-up price of 10%. In this way, the farmer was encouraged to work hard and save money for the grain purchasing. A field cultivated by a farmer can yield sixty *hu* (approximately 12.2 gallons) of grain every year. Within several years, the grain will be stored and the people will become rich".

This is the strategy of building granaries for the people's security.

The Emperor Zhuang of the Northern Wei dynasty built granaries for the people issuing an order to grant those who handed in grain an official rank.

In *Food Commodities· Book of Wei,* it is said that "in the early years of the Emperor Xiaozhuang (528 AD), national chaos resulted in an empty treasury and exhausted grain storage, consequently the law of buying official positions by grain was promulgated. Those who hand in 8000 *dan* of grain to the government earn the title of Sanhou; and 6000 *dan* donors become Sanbo. The incumbent officials who hand in 700 *dan* grain could be promoted to a higher rank of position involving actual work. The monks of Buddhist temples who pay 4000 *dan* to the Jing granary could be awarded the governor of the state where he comes from".

Such was the policy of giving grain for official posts.

这是纳粮卖官维持活命之策。

3. 隋唐时期

历史上，隋朝仅存在38年，开国者隋文帝在位24年，暴君隋炀帝杨广在位14年。隋朝历史虽短，但是隋文帝杨坚致力于社会稳定并重视粮食生产，所以粮食收成倍增，兴置大粮仓功绩举世公认。

隋朝首创赈灾义仓。

《隋书·食货志》载："开皇五年（公元585年）五月，工部尚书襄阳县公长孙平奏曰：古者三年耕而余一年之积，九年作而有三年之储，虽水旱为灾，而人民无菜色。……于是奏令诸州百姓及军人，劝课当社，共立义仓。收获之日，随其所得，劝课出粟及麦，于当社造仓窖贮之。"

《隋书·食货志》载，当时隋朝各州全都兴置了粮仓，其中最著名的粮仓有：卫州黎阳仓，在今河南淇县；洛州河阳仓，在今河南孟津县；陕州常平仓，在今河南陕县；华州广通仓，在今陕西华县；长安太仓，在今陕西西安市；隋朝兴建洛口仓和回洛仓。

近300年的唐朝历史是中国封建社会中的极盛时代，但李渊于长安

3. Sui and Tang Dynasties

During the 38 years of the Sui dynasty, the founding Emperor Wen of Sui dynasty had reigned for 24 years and the tyrant Yang Guang governed for 14 years. Although Sui dynasty was relatively short-lived, the Emperor Yang Jian was consistently committed to social stability and attached importance to grain production. Therefore, the achievements of doubling grain harvest and building large granaries were highly praised.

The Sui dynasty initiated the Yi granary for disaster prevention.

Food Commodities· Book of Sui records: "In the fifth year of the Emperor Wen of the Sui dynasty (585 AD), an official named Zhangsun Ping wrote that, in ancient times, three years of farming produced the grain savings for one-year storage, and the nine years of farming provided for three years of reserves. In this way, in the occurrence of floods or droughts, the farmer would not go hungry. It was with this in mind that I asked for the emperor's approval for an edict to encourage the farmers and soldiers to hand in grain to the community and set up public granaries together. In the harvest season, the farmers were persuaded to donate an amount of millet and wheat in proportion to their harvests to the community where the granaries and cellars were built for storage."

Food Commodities·Book of Sui records that granaries were built in all the states in the Sui dynasty. The most well-known granaries were the Liyang granary in Weizhou (now located in Qi county, Henan province), the Heyang granary in Luozhou (now located in Mengjin county, Henan province), the Changping granary in Shanzhou (now located in Shan county, Henan province), the Guangtong granary of Huazhou (now located in Hua county, Shaanxi province), the Taicang granary of Chang'an (now located in Xi'an city, Shannxi province), and the Luokou granary and the Huiluo granary built in the Sui dynasty.

The 300-year reign of the Tang dynasty spanned the golden days of China's feudal society. However, after Li Yuan proclaimed himself emperor in Chang'an, since the country was still unstable, there were no remarkable achievements in grain production for a long period of time.

By the Kaiyuan period of Li Longji, Emperor Xuanzong of the Tang dynasty, and following a hundred-year period of precarious harvests, good harvests began to lead to an abundance of grain. The old granaries were revitalized and new

称帝后的很长一段时间，其实社会仍然不稳定，所以，粮食生产长期没有突出的成就出现。

到了唐玄宗李隆基开元时期，唐朝饱经沧桑已经百年，粮食收成才初见富足，旧粮仓重振生机，新粮仓开始增加。

《旧唐书·食货志》载："十八年（公元730年），宣州刺史裴耀卿上便宜事条曰：从黄河不入漕洛，即于仓内安置。爰及河阳仓、柏崖仓、太原仓、永丰仓、渭南仓，节级取便，例皆如此。"

在以上史料中，永丰仓即广通仓、河阳仓和洛口仓等，前面已经讨论过。其他没有讨论到的粮仓，概括如下：太原仓，在今河南三门峡市陕州区；渭南仓，在今陕西渭南市；武牢仓及河口仓，在今郑州巩义市；河阴仓，在今郑州荥阳市；含嘉仓，在今洛阳市内。

四、社会公益储备

粮食储备承担着备荒、备战、扶困济贫等维系国计民生各个方面的全能职责。随着社会的发展，公益性的粮食储备随之兴起，为储粮领域增加了新的主体成员。由此出现了各种不同规模、功用、建筑形状和经营主体的储粮形式，逐渐形成了一个庞大的仓廪系统，在历史上产生了深刻影响，发挥了巨大作用。

历史上民间或社区设立的储备粮仓有义仓、社仓、学田仓等。这种社会公益性储粮形式历久不衰，在很长的历史时期内为民解困、为国分忧，发挥了良好的社会效益。清康熙十八年（公元1679年），始将设于乡村的

granaries began to appear.

Food Commodities· Book of Old Tang Dynasty records that "in the 18th year of the reign of Emperor Xuanzong of the Tang dynasty (730 AD), Pei Yaoqing, the prefectural governor of Xuanzhou, believed that ships from the Yellow River could unload grain into the Luokou granary for storage instead of entering the Luo River. It is traditional and convenient that grain is sequentially stored in the Heyang granary, the Baiya granary, the Taiyuan granary, the Yongfeng granary, and the Weinan granary".

In above data from ancient records, the Yongfeng granary comprises the Guangtong granary, the Heyang granary and the Luokou granary. Other granaries distributed in different provinces include the Taiyuan granary, now in Shan district, Sanmenxia city, Henan province; the Weinan granary, now in Weinan city, Shaanxi province; the Wulao granary and the Hekou granary in present-day Gongyi, Zhengzhou city; the Heyin granary in Xingyang, Zhengzhou city; and the Hanjia granary in present-day Luoyang city.

IV. Public Welfare Grain Reserve

Grain reserves play an all-round role in the prevention of famine and wars, the elimination of poverty, as well as in maintaining the national economy and improving people's livelihoods. The development of society depends on the essential role of public welfare grain reserves. It is for this reason that over the course of time, various forms of grain storage or ranging different scales, functions, architectural shapes and business models emerged, gradually forming a huge warehouse system with profound historical implications.

Historically, the reserve granaries which were set up by the people or communities were composed of Yi granary, She granary and Xuetian granary. The age-old system of social public welfare grain storage has been a true benefit for people and the nation alike. In the 18th year of the reign of Emperor Kangxi of the Qing dynasty (1679 AD), public welfare granaries located in the countryside were called She granaries, while those located in the city were called Yi granaries. In terms of their functions and purposes they were essentially the same.

公益粮仓称为社仓，设在城市的称为义仓，二者的功能和服务对象并无大的差别。

1. 义仓

义仓通常在县衙治所设置，具有半官方性质。相传隋朝开皇三年（公元 583 年），隋文帝诏令每年秋天每户农民捐出粟麦一石，储之间巷，以备凶年，名曰义仓。唐太宗贞观二年（公元 628 年），复有义仓之置，王公以下百姓亩纳粟二升，以备灾年赈济。元代仁宗时期，公元 1317 年，朝廷命各县置义仓，健全备荒济民体系。义仓由官方或民间机构管理，用于赈灾救济。

丰图义仓院落
The Countyard of Fengtu Yi Granary

1. Yi Granary

Yi granary was usually set up by the county administrative government and it was semi-official in nature. Legend has it that in the third year of the first emperor of the Sui dynasty (583 AD), Emperor Wen of the Sui dynasty ordered

丰图义仓
Fengtu Yi Granary

丰图义仓位于大荔县朝邑镇,由时任清朝东阁大学士的阎敬铭倡议修建。始建于1882年,1885年建成,慈禧太后朱批"天下第一仓",是目前中国唯一保存完好且仍在储粮的清代粮仓,2006年被确定为中国重点文物保护单位,现存中央储备粮5000吨。

浙江杭州富义仓遗址
Fu Yi Granary in Hangzhou, Zhejiang Province

浙江杭州富义仓,始建于清代光绪年间,位于杭州市霞湾巷8号京

each family to donate one *dan* (about 120 *jin*; 60kg) of millet and wheat each autumn and store them in the neighborhood lanes to prepare for a famine year, hence the name of Yi granary. In the second year of the reign of Emperor Taizong of the Tang dynasty (628 AD), the Yi granary was restored, and the people below title of princes and dukes were required to donate 2 liters of millet per acre for famine. During the reign of Emperor Renzong of the Yuan dynasty, in 1317, the court ordered the counties to set up Yi granaries in preparation for famine and the relief of the people's hardships. Yi granaries were managed by official or private organizations for disaster relief.

Located in Chaoyi town, Dali county, Fengtu Yi granary was built on the initiative of Yan Jingming, a grand secretary of the Qing dynasty. It was started in 1882 and completed in 1885, and was lauded as "the best granary in the world" by the Empress Dowager Cixi. Today, Fengtu Yi granary is the only Qing dynasty granary that is said to be well preserved. It is still in use for storing grain. In 2006, it was identified as a key cultural relic to be protected. It houses 5,000 tons of central grain reserves.

Fu Yi granary, built in the Guangxu period of the Qing dynasty and located beside the Beijing-Hangzhou Grand Canal, at No.8 Xiawan alley in Hangzhou, was the cornerstone of the Qing dynasty's national strategic grain storage system.

Yingyi Yi granary in Shenzhou, Hebei Province was abandoned after a long lapse of time.

河北深州盈亿义仓
Yingyi Yi Granary in Shenzhou, Hebei Province

杭大运河畔，是清代国家战略粮食储备仓库。

河北深州盈亿义仓，位于河北省深州市，由于年深日久，现已被废弃。

2. 社仓

社仓一般设置在村镇，是农村社区民办的公益性粮仓。库存粮食来源于劝捐或募捐，用于农民存丰补欠。社仓之名出现于隋，是官方义仓的延伸。后来，地方士绅和殷实望族将部分余粮贮备于仓，以资助村社孤寡，从而成为以粮食救济为物质基础的民间慈善机构的雏形。南宋时，由于政府的倡导和社会贤达的呼应，义仓真正具备了民间慈善机构的性质。其时，朱熹提出把赈灾储粮放在民间乡里，管理权仍属官方，既可解决"山谷细民，无盖藏之积，新陈未接，虽乐岁不免出倍称之息，贷食豪右"的弊害，又能防止"官粟积于无用之地，后将红腐不复可食"的损失。他身体力行，于乾道七年（1171年）在五夫首创了社仓。

潘氏社仓遗址
Panshi She Granary Site

深州盈亿义仓
Yingyi Yi Granary in Shenzhou

盈亿义仓内景
The Interior of Yingyi Yi Granary

2. She Granary

She public welfare granaries run by the non-government rural communities were usually set up in villages and towns. The grain in stock was donated and given to farmers to help them make up for poor harvest. The She granary first appeared in the Sui dynasty and was an extension of the publicly operated Yi granary. Later, the local gentry and wealthy families stored part of the surplus grain in the granary to support the orphans and widows of the village. Such practices represent the beginning of China's non-governmental charitable organizations for food relief. In the Southern Song dynasty, thanks to the guidance of the government, it became real non-governmental charitable institution. At that time, Zhu Xi proposed that grain storage for famine relief should be stored in the villages and

在传统的称谓概念里,有时社仓并不特指某个粮仓,而是指一种储粮制度。因为一些社仓并没有专门的仓库,只是利用祠堂或庙宇储藏粮食,待下一轮时就可能另辟新址。

朱熹建五夫社仓
She Granary in Wufu built by Zhu Xi

五夫社仓

She Granary in Wufu

3. 学田仓

学田指书院和州县官办学校所用的田地，是古代社会办学的经济来源之一，收贮学田租谷的仓廪称为学田仓。辟公田为"学田"、辟公禾为"学谷"的传统在中国有着悠久的历史。这种学田赡学制度初见于南唐，宋真宗乾兴元年（公元1022年）开始推广。学田的来源，或由皇帝诏赐，或由官府从官田中拨给，或由地方拨款购置，或由私人捐献。明代的学田制度获得很大发展，中国学田达数十万亩。到清代乾隆时，已经超过100万亩。各地学田一直延续到新中国成立之前。

官学田由督学官员管理，私学田由乡绅地主管理，有的也由学校生员管理。学田一般就近出租给当地农民耕种，每年按例收取田租。随着商品经济的发展，学田赡学的实物租改为了货币租，后来，学田仓逐渐退出历史舞台，至今遗迹无存。

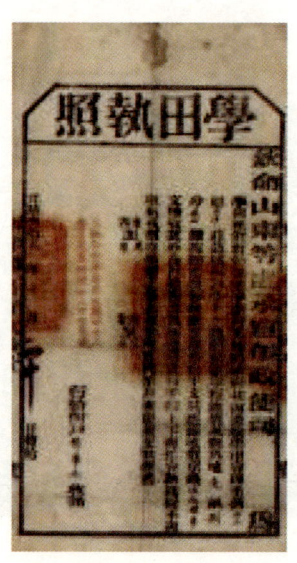

清代学田承租执照
Lease License of Xuetian in the Qing Dynasty

the government should enjoy the management rights. This would not only solve "the villagers' issue of shortage of grain and the high interest handed in to the landlord", but also prevent the loss of "officials having surplus grain, resulting in the rotten and wasteful grain". Zhu Xi practiced what he preached, and in the seventh year of Qiandao (1171 AD) he initiated She granary in Wufu.

She granary refers to a type of grain storage system. Since some She granaries do not have special warehouses, the grain can only be stored in ancestral halls or temples. Sometimes new locations are chosen for storage with each harvest.

3. Xuetian Granary

Xuetian, literally "studying land", refers to the land occupied by the academies, and the state and county authorities for the opening of government-run schools. Xuetian land was leased to provide the economic income for government-operated schools in ancient society. Xuetian granary stored grain harvest from the Xuetian lands. With a long traditional history in China, public lands and millet setup were separately called "Xuetian" and "Xuegu". The Xuetian system that first originated in the Southern Tang dynasty became widespread in the first year of the Qianxing period (1022 AD) of Emperor Zhenzong's reign in the Song dynasty. School lands were designated by imperial decree, allocated from the public land by the government, purchased by local government appropriations, or donated by individuals. In the Ming dynasty, the Xuetian system flourished and accounted for hundreds of thousands of *mu* (0.165 acres), and by the time of Emperor Qianlong of Qing dynasty, exceeded 1 million *mu*. The Xuetian system had continued right up until the founding of the People's Republic of China.

Public Xuetian was run by superintendents, while private Xuetian was overseen by the gentry landowners, and some by school students. Xuetian land was usually rented out to local farmers, usually with annual rent payments. The development of the commodity economy saw the payment in kind system replaced by currency rent payments. With the passing of time, the Xuetian granary gradually withdrew from the stage of history without any remains.

五、政府粮食储备

早在西周时期，人们就已经认识到了粮食仓储的重要作用，并将其作为统治者管理国家的一种重要手段和工具。《礼记·王制》载："国无九年之蓄曰不足，无六年之蓄曰急，无三年之蓄曰国非其国也。"《韩非子·显学》载："征赋钱粟，以实仓库。"古代官办粮食仓廪体制，主要设置有正仓、太仓、转运仓、常平仓等。

1. 正仓

正仓设置于州郡，由地方官府管理。

2. 太仓

太仓是设置于京都的王室粮仓，由最高统治者直接掌握，即所谓的皇家粮仓，主要为皇室和京官供应粮食。《越绝书》称："武王未下车，封比干之墓，发太仓之粟，以赡天下。"《史记·平准书》也有"汉兴七十余年之间，国家无事……太仓之粟，陈陈相因，充溢露积于外，致腐败不可食"的记载。

清代北京的皇家粮仓，规模庞大，设点集中，布局规整，发挥了保障皇室京师粮食供应的重要作用。清初承接了明朝遗留的7座皇家京仓，它们均集中在朝阳门附近，分别是海运仓、北新仓、南新仓、旧太仓、兴平仓、富新仓、禄米仓。乾隆年间，又增建了万安仓、太平仓、裕丰仓、储济仓、本裕仓和丰益仓等6座京仓。新旧太仓合称"京师十三仓"。此外，朝廷还在通州漕运中转码头建有中、西两座中央粮仓。因此，史上所称的"京通二仓"实际上是京城和通州两处中央粮库群的通称。

Ⅴ. Government Grain Reserve

As early as in the Western Zhou dynasty, people had realized the importance of grain storage, which was regarded as a crucial component for a ruler's governance. *The System of the King • The Book of Rites* explains: "It will be insufficient if a country's grain reserves can only be used for less than nine years; it will be urgent if less than six years. If the supply will not last three years, it will be disaster." *Famous School • Han Feizi* points out the need "to levy money and millet for the abundant grain reserve". The government-run grain storage system of ancient times mainly consisted of Zheng granary, Tai granary, Zhuanyun granary, and Changping granary.

1. Zheng Granary

Zheng granary, set up in the prefectures and counties, was managed by the local government.

2. Tai Granary

Tai granary is the royal granary located in the capital and controlled directly by the supreme ruler. It mainly provided grain for the royal family and the imperial officials. *The Book of Yue Jue* records, "Before coming to the throne, the Emperor Wu started to build the grave for Bigan escorted with the princes, and ordered the opening of Tai granary for the people's relief from hunger." *Pingzhun Book • Records of the Grand Historian* explains that "since the founding of the Han dynasty, there had been no upheavals in the country for more than 70 years…Grain in the Tai granary was such a state of abundance that the grains spilled out from the granary, rotten and inedible".

The imperial granary in Beijing of the Qing dynasty, with its large scale, centralized locations and orderly layout, played a crucial role guaranteeing the grain supply to the imperial capital. In the early Qing period, seven imperial granaries were inherited from the Ming dynasty, all of which surrounded Chaoyang Gate, respectively Haiyun granary, Beixin granary, Nanxin granary, Jiutai granary, Xingping granary, Fuxin granary and Lumi granary. During the reign of Emperor Qianlong, six imperial granaries were built, including Wan'an granary, Taiping granary, Yufeng granary, Chuji granary, Benyu granary, and Fengyi granary. The older and the newer Tai ganaries are collectively known as the

北京南新仓
Nanxin Granary in Beijing

3. 转运仓

转运仓是在运河沿线漕运重要节点兴建的粮仓，其职能是收储漕运粮食，及时向太仓转运，以保障安全便利地供应禄廪，补足军饷。

4. 常平仓

常平仓是国家粮食贮备仓，其职能是调节粮食供求，平抑市场粮价，救灾度荒，维护社会安定。汉宣帝五凤四年（公元前54年），大司农中丞耿寿昌力推设立官营粮食商业，筑仓储粮。此后，历代一直借鉴沿袭，使之成为国家一项重要的粮食储备制度，发挥了治国安民的突出作用。

部分常平仓遗址
Partial Ruins of Changping Granary

"Thirteen Capital Granaries". In addition, two central granaries of the imperial court were built in the middle and west of the Tongzhou water transport wharf. The so-called "Two Jingtong Granaries" refer to the two central grain storage clusters in central Beijing and its suburb of Tongzhou.

3. Zhuanyun Granary

Zhuanyun granary is a grain warehouse built at the key grain transport hub along the canal. Its function was to collect, store and transfer grain to Tai granary in time to guarantee the secure and unimpeded supply of grain and army provisions.

4. Changping Granary

As the national granary, the function of Changping granary is to regulate supply and its demand in the local grain trade, stabilize the grain prices, relieve famine, and maintain social stability. In the fourth year of the Wufeng Period of Emperor Xuan's rule in the Han dynasty (54 BC), the financial official Geng Shouchang implemented the policy of government-run grain commerce and built

部分常平仓遗址
Partial Ruins of Changping Granary

部分常平仓遗址
Partial Ruins of Changping Granary

5. 预备仓

预备仓是明朝初年开始设立的备荒粮仓。公元 1368 年，朝廷拨款 200 万贯作为籴本购买粮食，在居民集中住所设预备仓储粮，专备赈济之用。岁歉散发，秋后归还。

6. 营仓

营仓是清代专供兵士借贷的粮仓，一般设于边塞重镇，其谷本由政府拨付，各营将备经营。储粮规模按兵员数额大体保持每兵一至二石，士兵需粮时，或借或平粜。待秋后或兵士发饷时归还，不收利息。

7. 卫仓

卫仓是明代设于卫所驻防地的粮仓。当时京师和各地均设卫所，地方数府大抵 5600 名军士划为一个防区设卫，卫所中的军士大部分屯田，小部分驻防。明成祖（1403 年）时曾设天津卫仓和通州左卫仓，以及北京三十七卫仓，以保障卫所军粮的供给。

Changping granary for this purpose. Subsequent dynasties carried its forward initiative, and so it became one of the nation's most important grain reserve systems, and played a critical role in the exercise of the governance of China, and safeguarding its citizens.

5. Yubei Granary

Yubei granary was built in order to prepare against natural disasters in the early Ming dynasty. In 1368, the imperial court allocated 2 million *guan* (ancient currency in China; 1 *guan* was approximately equal to 90 *yuan* in modern China) to buy grain and set up Yubei granary to protect local residents against the famine. In famine years, grain from the Yubei granary was distributed to the residents and could be returned after the next harvest.

6. Ying Granary

Ying granary, generally located in key border towns, provided grain loans to soldiers during the Qing dynasty. The grain of Ying granary is funded by the government and reserved by each battalion. There was about one to two *dan* of grain to guarantee each soldier depending on the number of soldiers. The soldiers would either borrow or buy the grain when they needed and would pay for the grain interest-free after harvest or when they were paid.

7. Wei Granary

Wei granary was set up in garrisons in the Ming dynasty. At that time, the garrison posts were set up universally in the capital and in every other state. In local prefectures, one garrison area contained about 5,600 soldiers, most were stationed on farms, and a small number were stationed in the garrison. In 1403, the Emperor Ch'eng-tsu (Zhu Di) of the Ming dynasty set up Tianjin Wei granary, Tongzhou Zuowei granary and Beijing 37 Wei granary to guarantee the supply of military grain.

二战区（山西克难坡）军粮仓库牌
Military Granary Card from the Second War Area (Kenanpo, Shanxi Province)

六、历代著名粮仓

1. 百万石仓

百万石仓是秦汉时期（公元前200余年）储粮规模巨大的大粮仓。程敦《秦汉瓦当文字续》中载有"百万石仓"瓦当，并注明"瓦出汉旧城"，充分佐证了中国秦汉时期就有百万石大粮仓的史实。

2. 秦置敖仓

古代，中原地区战事频仍。秦始皇统一中国后，便在郑州附近的荥阳敖山置仓积谷，取名敖仓。敖仓兼有太仓和转运仓的双重角色，负责将经黄河运来的山东漕粮转运至长安、洛阳。由于当时黄河郑州以上河道水浅船滞，故需在敖仓卸粮暂储，改用陆路运抵两京。西汉重修敖仓，设置专官管理仓务，直属中央。据史载，汉武帝宠幸的王夫人请求封其子为洛阳王，武帝不允，曰："洛阳有武库、敖仓，当关口，天下

VI. Famous Granaries through the Ages

1. Baiwandan Cang—The "million *dan*" granary

Baiwandan (The "million *dan*" granary) is a large-scale granary used by the Qin and Han dynasties (200 BC). Cheng Dun's *Continuation of Qin and Han's Eaves Tile Characters* records the eaves tile from a "million *dan* warehouse" noting "the eaves are from the old city of Han dynasty". The tiles prove the existence of such a million *dan* granary in China during the Qin and Han dynasties.

2. Ao Granary in the Qin Dynasty

In ancient times, frequent wars took place in the Central Plains. Ao granary was established in Aoshan, Xingyang, close to Zhengzhou city, soon after the first emperor of the Qin dynasty unified China. Ao granary also carried out the dual function of Tai and Zhuanyun granaries. It was involved in the transfer of the grain shipment from Shandong to Chang'an and Luoyang via the Yellow River. Grain was temporarily unloaded and stored in the Ao granary, then transported to Chang'an and Luoyang by land, as the Yellow River water upstream from Zhengzhou was too shallow for shipment. During the period of the Western Han dynasty, the Ao granary was rebuilt and special officials who were directly affiliated with the central government were appointed to manage the granary. It is recorded that, Emperor Wu of the Han dynasty refused the request from his wife to grant their son the title of the king of Luoyang, saying that: "The military depot and the Ao granary are located in Luoyang, so Luoyang represents one of the nation's strategic passes, home to a vital. It had been inherited tradition initiated by the previous emperor that the title of king should not be granted in Luoyang." Such was the importance of the Ao Granary.

3. Jingshi Granary in the Han Dynasty

Located in Huayin City, Shaanxi Province, the Jingshi granary, also known as Hua granary, was built during the reign of Emperor Wu of the Han dynasty as a large national granary for storing and transporting grain for the capital Chang'an. But according to the terrain on which it lies, Jingshi granary is rectangular, 1,120 meters long from east to west and 700 meters long from north to south. Six granaries have been discovered at the Jingshi granary site, inside which the No.1 granary covers an area of 1,662.5 square meters with a storage capacity of 10,000

咽喉。自先帝以来，传不为置王。"可见敖仓地位之重要。

3. 汉置京师仓

京师仓位于陕西华阴市，又名华仓，建于汉武帝时期，是为首都长安储存、转运粮食的国家大型粮仓。京师仓依自然地势构筑，平面为长方形，东西 1120 米、南北 700 米。考古发现其中有粮仓 6 座，一号仓面积 1662.5 平方米，仓容量达上万立方米。由此可见，京师仓是一个浩大的粮食储备中转物流中心，是迄今发现的规模最大的西汉粮仓建筑。

4. 隋置回洛仓

回洛仓城遗址位于隋唐洛阳城外的东北部，南距隋唐洛阳城外郭城北城墙 1000 米，地势平坦开阔，不易积水。2004 年 9 月，文物工作者发现了这处著名的粮仓。

史料记载，隋炀帝迁都洛阳的同时，在洛阳城北修建回洛仓，作为供应东都粮食的储备仓库。回洛仓隋末被瓦岗军占领。《隋书·食货志》记载：大业元年（公元 605 年），"炀帝即位……始建东都……每月役丁二百万人。徙洛州部内人及天下诸州富商大贾数万家，以实之。新置兴洛及回洛仓"。对回洛仓的位置和规模，《资治通鉴》卷一八〇记载："炀帝大业二年十二月，置回洛仓于洛阳北七里，仓城周回十里，穿三百窖。"《文献通考》卷二五"国用考"记载：大业年间，"置洛口回洛仓，穿三千三百窖，窖容八千"。

回洛仓城遗址与大运河申遗有着密切的关系。回洛仓是隋朝大型国家粮仓，是大运河沿线重要的粮仓遗址，是以洛阳为枢纽的隋唐大运河的实物例证之一，也是隋代修建大运河的主要目的之一。

目前已发掘出仓窖 7 座，其形制基本相同，均呈口大底小的圆缸形。仓窖的修建是从地面向下先挖一个口大底小的圆缸形土窖，窖壁和底部经过细致加工，平整光滑。在仓窖挖成以后，进行防潮处理。考古发现仓窖的周壁和底部保留有木板和黑灰以及火烧过的"防潮层"。

cubic meters. Thus, it can be seen that the Jingshi granary is the largest known granary of the Western Han dynasty.

京师仓一号仓
No.1 Jingshi Granary

4. Huiluo Granary in the Sui Dynasty

The city site of Huiluo granary, discovered by antiquarians in September of 2004, was located at the northeast of Luoyang city during the Sui and Tang dynasties, 1,000 meters south to the north wall of Luoyang city. One of the key features of Huiluo granary is that it could carry out water drainage thanks to the surrounded flat and wide terrain.

According to historical records, when the Emperor Yang of Sui dynasty moved the capital to Luoyang, he built Huiluo granary in the north of Luoyang city to serve as a storage warehouse to supply grain to the eastern capital. According to *Food Commodities · Sui Geographical Chronicles*: "In the first year of Daye (605 AD), when Emperor Yang of the Sui dynasty came to the throne and established the eastern capital in Luoyang, each month saw another two million young men enrolled in the task to build the capital. The residents of Luozhou city and tens of thousands of wealthy merchants from various states immigrated to Luoyang, where Xingluo granary and Huiluo granary were built." *Zizhi Tongjian* (Volume 180) records that "in December of the 2nd year of Daye,

仓窖的形制结构
The Shape of Warehouse Cellar

仓窖的建筑和防潮处理大致可分为以下几个步骤。第一步，在地面上挖一个直壁环形基槽，外直径不小于 16 米，内直径不小于 10 米，深 1.3–1.7 米，并对环形基槽进行夯打，以此作为防水、防塌坚实的仓窖口；然后将环形基槽内的土挖出，形成口部直径 10 米、底部直径 7–8 米、深 7–8 米的口大底小呈圆缸形的仓窖。第二步，对仓窖壁进行简单拍打，然后用火烧烤窖壁面，使之完全干燥。第三步，对整个仓窖壁加铺厚 20 厘米的青膏泥，用以防渗漏。第四步，在青膏泥防渗层上加铺一层木板，再在木板上铺一层竹席。最后再存放粮食。

因受长年的雨水冲刷，仓窖口塌落严重，原建筑遗迹已无存，窖顶的外形和具体建筑情况也无从知晓。但《王祯农书》中详细记载了农民仓储粮食的方法："夫穴地为窖，小可数斛，大至数百斛，先令柴棘，烧投其土焦燥，然后周以糠，稳贮粟于内。"回洛仓就是采用此种储藏的方法。

储藏漕粮的数量，以 3 号仓窖为例推算：窖口直径 10 米，底直径 7 米，深 7 米，该仓窖体积 401.135 立方米。仓窖中粮食所占的体积约

the Emperor Yang of the Sui dynasty established Huiluo granary seven *li* (about 3,500 meters) away from Luoyang in the north, and it covered an area of more than 10 square miles, housing 300 cellars in total". According to the *National Examination* (Volume 25 of *A Critical History of Institutions*): "During the period of Daye, the Huiluo granaries were established at the mouth of Luokou, comprising 3,300 cellars and having a grain capacity of 8,000 *dan*."

Huiluo granary is a large-scale national granary in Sui dynasty and an indispensable granary of the Grand Canal. It is was central to China's successful application for the Grand Canal to be listed as a world heritage site. Additionally, it is also one of the physical cases of the Grand Canal of Sui and Tang dynasties with Luoyang as the hub, and one of the reasons behind the construction of the Grand Canal of Sui dynasty.

Up to today, 7 warehouse cellars have been excavated, and all are round cylinders with large mouths and small bottoms. To build a warehouse cellar, a cylinder-shaped underground cave should be delicately dug into the ground, which has a wide mouth and a small bottom. The cellar's wall and the bottom should have been polished delicately. Until they are polished smooth, the moisture-proofing should be carried out. The archeological digging found wooden boards, ash, and the burnt fire-baked moisture-proofing on the wall and bottom of the cellars.

The construction and moisture-proofing of the cellar can be roughly divided into the following steps. First, vertical walled and circular ditch must be dug with an outer diameter of not less than 16 meters, and an inner diameter not less than 10 meters. It must be between 1.3 and 1.7 meters in depth. Then the foundation ditch must be tamped as it will become the granary's mouth. The mouth must be waterproof and solid to prevent collapse. Afterwards, the soil must be dug out to form a cellar with a 10 meters wide mouth, 7-8 meters in diameter base, and a depth of 7-8 meters. The second step is to pat and fire-bake the cellar wall to dry it completely. The third step is to daub the wall of the cellar with 20 cm thick green mud paste to prevent leakage. The fourth step is to add a layer of wood on mud daubing before and then spread a layer of bamboo onto the wood. The last step is to add the grain.

The original structure had not been discovered until recently because years

为 344 立方米。稻米和粟米的比重为：每立方米 0.8 吨，仓窖中可储粮 275 吨，即当年每座仓窖大约储放粮食 55 万斤。目前钻探出该仓城有仓窖 700 座左右，总储粮大约 1.93 亿公斤，数量十分惊人。

5. 唐建含嘉仓

含嘉仓位于洛阳西北部，隋大业元年（公元 605 年）初建。隋末东都洛阳的粮仓不集中，洛口、回洛等仓被占据后，洛阳终因严重乏粮而被攻破。李世民显然看准了粮仓远离洛阳庇护的弊端，从隋末战乱中吸取了教训。唐代初年，洛阳城内出现了一座大粮仓，并逐渐取代洛口仓，成为天下第一大粮仓。这就是中国古代最著名的大粮仓——含嘉仓。含嘉仓占地面积 43 万平方米，共有圆形仓 400 多个，大窖可储粮 1 万石以上，小窖可储粮数千石。仓群规模宏大，仓体结构完善，显示了当时的建仓技术已经达到相当高的水平。大粮仓折射出"大唐盛世"，据记载，唐玄宗天宝八年（公元 749 年），中国主要大型粮仓的储粮总数为 1265 多万石，含嘉仓就达近 600 万石，占了约二分之一，可知其无与比肩的规模和地位。

含嘉仓刻铭砖
Brick with Inscriptions in Hanjia Granary

唐朝前期，洛口仓虽然仍是重要粮仓，但其地位逐渐为含嘉仓取

of rain-wash had caused the near-total collapse of the cellar's mouth. The shape of the pit roof and some of the specifics of its construction are still unknown. The *Wang Zhen Agricultural Book* records the methods of grain storage in detail. "The capacities of some granaries built underground are as small as several *hu*, and some are as large as several hundred. The farmer first burnt some firewood to dry the earth and then circled it with bran for the safe storage of the grain." This is the storage method that was applied in the case of Huiluo granary.

The quantity of the grain stored in No.3 cellar is calculated as follows: the mouth diameter of the cellar is 10 meters; the bottom diameter is 7 meters, and the depth is 7 meters. The volume of the cellar is 401.135 cubic meters, about 344 cubic meters of which stored the grain. The cellar stores 0.8 tons per cubic meter, and 275 tons in total, which means each year around 550 thousand *jin* of grain can be stored in each cellar. Recently came the astonishing discovery in which 700 cellars were excavated meaning a total grain storage capacity of 0.193 billion kilograms.

5. Hanjia Granary in Tang Dynasty

Located in the northwest of Luoyang, Hanjia granary was built in the first year of Daye period in the Sui dynasty. At the end of the Sui dynasty, the granaries in Luoyang, the eastern capital, were not at a centralized location. After the granaries of Luokou and Huiluo were occupied by enemies, Luoyang eventually fell due to a serious lack of grain. Li Shimin, the emperor of Tang dynasty, understood the disadvantages of keeping granaries far away from the capital Luoyang and learnt from the chaos of the late Sui dynasty. In the early Tang dynasty, a large granary was built in Luoyang city. It was in fact the largest granary in the country at the time, and would gradually replace Luokou granary. Hanjia granary, as the most famous granary in ancient China, covers an area of 430,000 square meters with over 400 circular granaries, the largest of which stored more than 10 thousand *dan* of grain, the smaller cellars could store several thousand *dan*. The large scale of this group granaries and the well-structured body is the testament to the fact that the technology for building granaries at that time was well-developed. The grand scale of Hanjia granary reflects the "prosperous period of the Tang dynasty". According to the historical records, in the eighth year of Tianbao, during the reign of Emperor Xuanzong in the Tang dynasty (749

代。含嘉仓的地位日益重要，它不仅是洛阳的粮仓，并且还起着关东和关中之间漕米转运站的作用。隋时东南漕米都先集中在洛口仓；唐前期则规定东都洛阳以东的租米都先集中在含嘉仓，由含嘉仓再陆运至陕州，循河、渭入长安。新兴的含嘉仓因此成为中国最大的粮仓。

含嘉仓的粮窖形制结构十分科学。粮窖都是口大底小的圆缸形。建造过程是先从地面向下挖成土窖，将窖底夯实，用火烧硬，然后铺一层用红烧土碎块和黑灰等拌成的混合物作为防潮层，防潮层上再铺一层木板层或木板和草的重叠混合层。含嘉仓的粮窖既能防潮防火，又能防鼠防盗。唐朝时窖内的谷子可藏 9 年，稻米可藏 5 年。160 号窖内的谷子至今已有 1300 多年了，颗粒还可辨认。经化验，这些炭化谷粒中有机物仍占 50.8%。

含嘉仓的管理也很科学，大部分窖内都发现了砖刻铭文，记载着窖穴的位置、编号、储粮来源、品种、数量、入窖年月等。含嘉仓的结构特点和规模表明，中国古代人民在隋唐时期就已掌握了相当科学的储粮技术。现在，国家将已发掘的 160 号粮窖建屋保护，作为中国现存古代最大粮窖的陈列馆。

2014 年，大运河在联合国申遗成功，回洛仓和含嘉仓都成功入选世界遗产名录。

AD), the total amount of grain stored in China's major granaries was over 12.65 million *dan*, 6 million of which was stored in Hanjia granary. Hanjia granary's scale and reputation was unparalleled in that age.

In the early Tang dynasty, Luokou granary, with its critical role, was gradually replaced by Hanjia granary. Hanjia granary was not only an important granary for Luoyang's grain storage, but also played the vital role of a river transfer station between Guandong (the east region of Hangu Pass) and Guanzhong (the central Shaanxi plain). In the Sui dynasty, river transportation of rice from the southeast was prepared in the Luokou granary. And in the Tang dynasty, rice paid as rent from the east of Luoyang was first prepared in the Hanjia granary, before being transported from Shanzhou to Chang'an along the Yellow and Weihe rivers. Therefore, it was the newly born Hanjia granary that became the largest one in China in its day.

The grain cellar of Hanjia granary, with its cylindrical shape, wide mouth, and small bottom, is excellently designed. Firstly, a soil cellar from underground is dug, tamping and firing the bottom of the cellar until it becomes hard, then a layer of the mixture of the fired clods and black dust is used to make as the moisture barrier, above which a layer of planking or a mixture of the planks and grass is placed. As a result, Hanjia granary is moisture-proof, fireproof, rat-proof, theft-proof. In the Tang dynasty, the millet in the cellar could be stored for 9 years and the rice for 5 years. Although the millet in the cellar of No.160 is over 1,300 years old, the particles are still recognizable. Chemical analysis shows that the organic material in these carbide grains accounts up for 50.8%.

Hanjia granary was especially well organized, for example, most cellar bricks have been found to have inscriptions that record the location, number, and source of grain storage, its variety, quantity, and even storage date. The structural characteristics and scale of Hanjia granary indicate that the ancient Chinese people had already mastered an advanced grain storage technology during the Sui and Tang dynasties. Nowadays China maintains the cellar No.160 of Hanjia granary and has turned it into the largest exhibition hall of ancient China.

In 2014, with the successful application of the Grand Canal to be listed as a World Heritage Site, both Huiluo granary and Hanjia granary were also entered into the World Heritage List.

6. 明置南京石头仓

明代洪武年间,在南京城内设置石头仓,用以储备军粮。

南京石头仓遗址(军储仓)
Stone Granary Site in Nanjing (Military Grain Granary)

7. 明置东门仓

明朝的中央粮仓主要是北京的东门仓(后称南门仓、南新仓)和通州仓。东门仓位于现今的东城区东四十条附近,是在元代北太仓基础上于1409年(明永乐七年)建造的,比建于1420年(明永乐十八年)的

6. Nanjing's Shitou (Stone) Granary in the Ming Dynasty

In the Hongwu years of the Ming dynasty, Stone granary was built in Nanjing for military grain storage.

7. Dongmen (East Gate) Granary in the Ming Dynasty

The central granaries in the Ming dynasty were mainly composed of the Dongmen granary (later called Nanmen granary and Nanxin granary) and Tongzhou granary in Beijing. Dongmen granary, located near Dongsishitiao in the present-day Dongcheng district of Beijing, was built in 1409 (the 7th year of Yongle in the Ming dynasty) on the site of the Beitai granary in the Yuan dynasty, 10 years before the construction of the Forbidden City (built in 1420, the 18th year of Yongle in the Ming dynasty). It is recognized as the largest and best-preserved granary complex in Chinese history. The granary has a height of 10 meters, a wall thickness of 1.5 meters, ventilation holes and skylights, with a constant temperature throughout the seasons, suitable humidity, and is impermeable to rodents. It is China's most primitive subject of ecological protection.

北京南新仓
Nanxin Granary in Beijing

故宫还年长十岁，为中国规模最大、保存最完好的历史仓敖实物建筑群。该仓高 10 米，墙体厚 1.5 米，设通气孔与天窗，四季恒温，湿度适宜，没有鼠患，是中国最原始的物理保护生态建筑。

北京皇家粮仓
Imperial Granary in Beijing

8. 清置丰图义仓

丰图义仓位于陕西大荔县，建在黄河西岸的一处台塬上，地势高兀，通风向阳，仓基土层干燥，利于粮食储存。该仓是一座仓城合一的城堡式建筑，分外城和内城，兼具防御和储粮双重功能。外城夯土筑

8. Fengtu Yi (Public) Granary in the Qing Dynasty

Fengtu Yi (Public) granary, located in Dali county, Shannxi province, was built on the loess platform of the west bank of the Yellow River. The high terrain, good ventilation, exposure to sufficient sunlight, and dry base soil layer are all conducive to grain storage. The granary is a castle-like building with inner and outer courtyards, affording it the dual capabilities of defense and grain storage. The outer courtyard was built with rammed earth and cliffs on three sides. The front door faces the west, and the back door faces the east. The inner courtyard represents a castle inside a castle, sitting north to south, with brick walls. Covering a total area of 11,039 square meters, the granary is 133 meters long from east to west, 83 meters wide from north to south, and about 8 meters high. The south wall opens with east and west doors. In the inner courtyard, 58 kilns are embedded around the warehouse wall to provide a total capacity of 5,220 tons.

Each kiln warehouse is made from bricks. They have a depth of 8 to 12 meters, a width of about 3.9 meters and a grain storage capacity of about 90 tons. The bottom of the kiln warehouse is paved with pine boards 40 cm above the ground. There are ventilation channels (also called cat holes) under the boards for ventilation, moisture drainage and rodent prevention, with small transoms on the top for natural ventilation. The kiln warehouse is equipped with two doors, the plug-in type inner layer, which can be removed to dehumidify when weather conditions require it. The brick and tile corridors outside are rainproof, moisture-proof and provide temporary storage space for the grain. The center of the warehouse is used for drying grain, south of which is the courtyard house. Two separate buildings slightly to the east and west provide the guards' working and living spaces.

The roof of the granary is covered with blue bricks, and the joints are bonded with glutinous rice juice, white lime, lime soil and slurry. The mixture is strong and rainwater-proof. The top of the granary is equipped with twelve drainage basins. Each one is high at the edges with a 25-degree slope to its base. Rainwater can be collected in the middle and discharged by the cast iron U-shaped channel, which skillfully solved the problem of drainage on the top of the granary. The water-guide wall supporting the U-shaped water channel extends 5 meters out of the granary and functions as a firewall. The roof of the granary is surrounded on

城，三面绝壁，城正门面西，东面有后门。内城为城中城，坐北向南，砖砌周垣，东西长 133 米，南北宽 83 米，高约 8 米，占地 11039 平方米，南壁洞开东仓门和西仓门。内城依仓墙环列窑仓 58 孔，总仓容 5220 吨。

每孔窑仓为独立的砖窑结构，进深 8－12 米不等，宽约 3.9 米，可储粮约 90 吨。窑仓底部由松木板铺成，距地面 40 厘米，木板下为通风道（也叫猫洞），可通风、排潮和防鼠，顶部还有小气窗自然通风。窑仓设两道门，里层为插板式，可依据天气情况打开除湿。窑仓外有砖瓦结构的廊房环绕，具有防雨、防潮及临时储粮功能。仓院中央是晾晒粮食的晒场。中轴线以南有四合院和东、西厦房各一座，旧时供守仓人办公及生活所用。

仓顶铺设青砖，糯米汁、白石灰、灰土和浆黏结嵌缝，结实坚固且防雨水渗漏。仓顶分十二段排水，每段都是中间低四周高，比降 25 度，可将雨水汇集中间，由铸铁 U 型水道排出，巧妙地解决了仓顶排水问题。支撑 U 型水道的导水墙伸出仓外 5 米，兼具防火墙的功能。仓顶四面环通，半人高的女儿墙护卫四周，具有防御作用。该仓仓墙、仓顶均为厚实的砖体结构，且防潮、通风效果良好，使窑仓具有冬暖夏凉的特点，一年四季处于约 20℃的恒温状态和低温、低湿、低氧的"三低"状态，粮食储存 5 年以上仍能保持原来品质。

丰图义仓历经百年风雨沧桑仍在为国储粮，在历次灾荒中，放粮赈济，救民无数，发挥了储粮救灾的重要作用。丰图义仓地形选择巧妙，建筑艺术高超，气势雄伟壮观，是中国粮仓建筑史上集防御和储粮功能于一体的生态建筑的典范，堪称古建筑之瑰宝，已成为大荔县重要的旅游景点之一。

all sides, and the half-person-height parapet guards the surroundings, which has a defensive effect. The thick-brick-structured walls and roof are such moisture proof and well ventilated that the kiln is warm in winter and cool in summer. Thanks to the low-oxygen, low-temperature, and low-humidity conditions inside the kiln, the grain can still maintain its original quality after more than 5 years of storage.

After thousands of years of turbulent history, Fengtu Yi granary is still storing grain today. It has provided food and saved countless people from famine, playing an indispensable role in grain storage and disaster relief. The choice of location for Fengtu Yi granary is a unique art and it is an architectural marvel in its grandeur. It is not only regarded as a typical model of ecological architecture, integrating defense and grain storage, but also as a gem of the ancient architecture which has become one of the most important tourist attractions in Dali county.

第二章

谷脉流长

Chapter 2

History of Grain Circulation

粮食流通贸易是粮食作为商品通过市场交换实现从生产领域向消费领域转移的过程。这种转移过程以货币为媒介，借助其流通职能和支付职能来实现。粮食流通是全社会商品流通的重要组成部分，对促进生产发展、保证市场供应、繁荣国民经济等方面都具有十分重要的意义。历史上，中国在粮食流通贸易领域铸就了一段段民殷国强的盛世辉煌，成为保障国家安定、社会发展和人民安居乐业的中坚力量。

现阶段，中国坚持立足国内实现粮食基本自给的方针，实行宏观调控下的市场调节，保持中国粮食供应总量基本平衡和价格基本稳定，呈现出粮食经营市场化、经营主体多元化、贸易交流国际化的局面。

一、粮食贸易探源

1. 以粮换粮、以粮换物的原始贸易

人类的原始公有制时期，不存在凌驾于氏族成员之上的统治者，部落成员内部也没有产生职业分工，因而不存在以采集来的野生谷物进行交换的经济行为。到新石器时代晚期，随着粮食种植业的产生和发展，公有制的氏族部落逐渐向私有制的奴隶社会过渡。私有财产的出现，促使部落成员之间包括粮食的物品交换行为也随之发生，这种进行交换的场所即被称为"市井"。

中国长期的农耕社会以自给自足的小农经济为主，人们的剩余粮食多用来自销。起初的粮食交易大多为粗换细的品种对换，或相对公平的粮物交换，间或少量民间余缺调剂和乡里街坊间的对等交换。当时，以粮换粮的主要形式有以粗换细、以秋换夏、以稻换麦、以薯换谷、以原粮换成品粮等。以粮换物的主要形式有以粮换兽皮、以粮换盐、以粮换铁、以粮换布、以粮换牲畜、以粮换其他副食品和蔬菜等。粮食作为商品进入流通领域是随着社会生产力的逐步提高和生产关系的改变，以及自然经济向商品经济转型发展起来的。

The grain circulation trade is a process in which grain as a commodity is transferred from the production to the consumption field through market exchange. With its function of circulation and payment, this transfer process is realized by using the currency as a medium. Grain circulation was an integral part of the commodity logistics throughout society and an essential part of development, trade, and national economy prosperity. Historically, with a glorious history, China's grain logistic trade has been as the backbone of the national stability, social development and the people's prosperity.

At the present stage, China adheres to the policy of achieving basic grain self-sufficiency domestically, implementing market regulation under macro-control, and maintaining a basic balance between supply and demand as well as the basic stability in prices. The management of grain is therefore diversified according to the nature of the global market.

Ⅰ. The Origins of Grain Trade

1. Early Grain for Goods

During humankind's era of primitive public ownership, there was no authoritative rule and occupational division of labor among clan members. It is for these reasons that grain exchange would not appear on the stage of history until sometime later. In the late Neolithic period, the appearance and development of grain plantations gradually transformed the publicly-owned clan and tribe and privately-owned slave society emerged. The emergence of private property prompted the exchange of goods, including grain among the tribal members. Such exchanges took place at the market.

In accordance with the nature of the self-sufficient small-scale farming economy of the time, Chinese farmers produced and sold their surplus grain by themselves. Early grain bargains mainly focused on exchanges between the coarse and fine grain varieties, or relatively fair grain exchanges, occasionally non-governmental surplus adjustments and reciprocal exchanges between villages and neighborhoods would take place. At that time, the most common grain for grain exchanges involved coarse grain for fine grain, autumn grain for summer grain, rice for wheat, potato for grain, and raw grain for possessed grain. Grain for food

2. 古代粮食市场交易

大约 5000 年前的新石器时代晚期，人们的粮食生产除满足自身需求外已有剩余，黄河流域的各部落出现了"日中为市"形式的物物交换的粮食交易。在进入奴隶社会后，由于城市的建立和手工业的发展，商业流通渐盛，粮食交易活动频繁，奴隶主在城中设"市"进行粮食交换，委任"司市"人员管理交易市场。这种新的经济形态发挥了流通的功能，适应了当时的社会发展，无论贵族还是普通百姓皆乐于此道，于是，以"商"为国号的政治架构随之产生。商朝开国之君汤组织妇女"文绣篡组"，换取夏人粮食，"一纯得粟百钟"。由此赋予了粮食商品交换的功能，开粮食贸易流通活动之先河。

卖红薯场景·辽宁博物馆
The Scene of Sweet Potatoes Bargain · Liaoning Museum

封建社会时期，粮食成为市场的主要商品之一，出现了定期进行交易的集市贸易，也有专司粮食交易的"米市"。战国时期，魏国的白圭曾为魏惠王的相国，后来转向买卖，经营的商品主要是粮食，被后世奉为"商人祖师"。从两汉到魏晋南北朝时期，城市经济迅猛发展，粮食贸易日益繁荣。《齐民要术·杂说》记载："凡籴五谷、菜子，皆需初熟

exchanges encompassed grain for animal skins, grain for salt, grain for iron, grain for cloth, grain for livestock, and grain for other nonstaple foods and vegetables. With the development of social productivity and the improvement of production relations, and the transformation of the natural economy into a commodity economy, grain was gradually becoming a commodity.

2. The Ancient Grain Market

In the late Neolithic period, about 5,000 years ago, people were already enjoying surplus grain production after satisfying their own needs for sustenance. The daytime trading business model appeared among the tribes of the Yellow River Basin. After the slave society had taken shape, the establishment of cities and the development of the handicraft trade spurred commercial circulation and a growth in the scale of grain trading. Slave owners set up markets where grain could be exchanged, appointing the "Sishi" to manage the market. This new economic model exerted the function of circulation and encouraged circulation, dovetailed with the trends of social development of the day. The markets were enjoyed and accepted by both the nobles and commoners alike. From then on, a political structure with commerce at its heart came into being. Tang, the founding emperor of the Shang dynasty, called for women to carry out "Embroidery and Weave" in exchange for the grain from Xia's people. Hence grain had become a commodity, which signaled the beginning of the grain trade.

During the days of feudal society, grain became one of the main market commodities. The bazaar was regularly open for grain trade alongside the specialized "rice market". During the Warring States period, Bai Gui served as the Prime Minister to Emperor Hui of Wei state, and he later tuned his talent to the bussiness of grain. From then on, he would be known as "the father of merchants". From the times of the Han dynasty to the Wei Jin Southern and Northern dynasties, the urban economy developed rapidly and the grain trade was increasingly prosperous. The ancient book of *Fragmentary Argumentation of Qi Min Yao Shu* records: "It is best to purchase grain when it first ripens and sell it in time for planting. In the same way, it is profitable for farmers to purchase beans and grains in winter and sell in summer and autumn of the flood season." It can be seen the practice of seeking fortune by means of the grain trade was very common. Wang Fu, a philosopher of Han dynasty, said that, at that time, there

日籴，将种时粜，收利必倍。凡冬籴豆、谷，至夏秋初雨潦之时粜之，价亦数倍之。"由此可见，当时北方粮食市场交易逐利行为已经普遍展开。汉代哲学家王符说，自己所处的时代，从事工商业者十倍于农民，集贸繁荣达到"牛马车舆，堵塞道路"的程度。唐代在长安东西两市都出现了"粮行"，固定铺面，规模化地经营粮食商业。在远僻的边境地区，官府开展了大批量的"和籴"行动，即国家出钱以市场价收购农民的粮食，以充边储。

中国历史上最繁荣的大都市出现在宋代，当时城市规模扩张，居民人口占到中国总人口 20% 以上，粮铺遍布街巷，保证了广大居民的生活供应。宋《梦粱录》记载："杭州人烟稠密，城内外居不下十万户，百十万口。每日街市食米，城内外不下一二千余石，皆需之铺家。"

明清时期，中国的经济规模处于世界第一，拥有最高的粮食产量，粮食贸易繁荣活跃，大小"米市"遍地开花。有些粮商经营规模庞大，交易繁荣，其中南方最著名的"四大米市"是江苏无锡米市、安徽芜湖米市、江西九江米市、湖南长沙米市。

古代都市场景·中国水利博物馆
The Scene of Ancient Market· National Water Museum of China

were ten times as many people engaged in industry and commerce than there were in farming, and the markets were so bustling and vibrant that the customer traffic would block up the roads. In the Tang dynasty, large scale grain shops of fixed address appeared in the east and west markets of Chang'an. In remote border areas, "Hedi" policy was rolled out whereby the government paid for grain at market prices to provide food for the frontier reserves.

The most prosperous metropolis in Chinese history appeared in the Song dynasty. At that time, urban resident population was quickly expanding to more than 20% of China's total population. Grain shops, scattered alongside the streets, guaranteed the food supply for the residents. The book *Menglianglu* of the Song dynasty records how "Hangzhou is densely populated, with more than 100,000 households and about one million residents living in and outside the city. Every day, the market provides over 2,000 *dan* of rice."

During Ming and Qing dynasties, China maintained its position as the world's largest economy with the highest grain output. The grain trade was prosperous and various rice markets blossomed. Some grain merchants engaged in large-scale profitable operations. The most famous four rice markets in the south were Wuxi Rice Market in Jiangsu province, Wuhu Rice Market in Anhui province, Jiujiang Rice Market in Jiangxi province, and Changsha Rice Market in Hunan province.

In the traditional grain market, "Diliang" and "Tiaoliang" refer to purchasing and selling grain respectively. They reflect the direct and pure nature of the ancient grain circulation. The in-out actions, although seemingly simple, reflect and embody the rich social reality, convey the cultural progress of humanity. The term "Ji" is used in the north and "Xu" in the south. "Chang" or "Xing" are used in the southwest. The terms "Shangji" and "Ganxu" derive from long usage in the vast rural areas.

芜湖米市雕塑
Statues in Wuhu Rice Market

　　传统粮食市场中,"籴粮"和"粜粮"是两种不同的交易概念,其实就是两种主体不同的买卖行为,反映了古代粮食流通交易的直接与纯粹。在看似简单的一进一出的两种行为中,反映着世情百态,包蕴着十分丰富的社会现象,传达了文明进步的人文信息。这种以粮食交易为主要内容的集市贸易形式,在北方称为"集",在南方称为"圩(墟)",西南地区则称为"场"或"行"。广大农村地区长期流行的"上集""赶圩(墟)"之说,即由此而来。

古代粮食贸易·中国财税博物馆
Ancient Grain Trade · China Finance and Taxation Museum

3. 古代粮食流通的国家管理

历代始终"视粟为国命",因而粮食流通一般都处于政府的管制和干预之下,国家常常采取"平粜""平籴"和"遏籴"等政策措施,对市场粮价进行统制,同时利用经济杠杆适时进行平抑。

毋遏籴盟约 春秋战国时期,各诸侯国的都城和市镇逐渐兴起,城居的非农业人口迅速增加。由于各地的粮食生产条件和经济发展不平衡,粮食供需方面出现了区域性的丰歉余缺,客观上促进了粮食的贩卖贸易。但是,一旦出现灾荒缺粮的危机,各诸侯国就会禁止粮食出口,即"遏籴",禁止别国前来本国购买粮食。这就使受灾严重的诸侯国雪上加霜,人们生活更加困难。为了禁止这种以邻为壑、无视他人安危的行径,公元前651年,最早称霸的齐桓公出面召集诸侯大会于葵丘(今河南兰考),与会者有鲁、宋、郑、卫、许、曹等国,周天子也派人前来参加会议。会上订立了"毋遏籴"盟约,约定各国都不能阻止受灾国到余粮国购买粮食。

齐桓公葵丘会盟场景·齐国历史博物馆
Meeting Scene in Kuiqiu · History Museum of Kingdom Qi

3. The National Management of the Ancient Grain Circulation

In former dynasties, millet was regarded as the lifeblood of the nations. Therefore, grain circulation was usually generally under the control and management of the government. Policies and leverage tools like "Pingtiao", "Pingdi" and "E'Di" were often adopted to control the market price of grain and maintain market equilibrium.

Wu E'Di Treaty During the Spring and Autumn and Warring States period, capitals and towns in the vassal states gradually emerged, with non-agricultural urban populations increasing rapidly. At that time, unbalanced regional economic development and grain production enabled a regional surpluses and shortages in the supply and demand of grain, which engendered the appearance of grain trade. However, following a grain shortage during a famine period many states started to prohibit the export of grain, this prohibition measure was called "E'Di" literally, which limited buying of others states. This kind of prohibition made life harder for the countries which were severely affected by the disaster. To put an end to the beggar-thy-neighbour effects of the E'Di policy, in 651 BC, Duke Huan of Qi convened a meeting attended by the dukes of various regional countries in Kuiqiu (present-day Lankao county, Henan province). The attendees included the dukes of Lu, Song, Zheng, Wei, Xu, Cao, as well as representatives dispatched by the Emperor Zhou. At the meeting, "Wu E'Di Treaty" was signed. The treaty stipulated that no state should prevent famine-striken countries from purchasing grain from states which were enjoying a surplus.

The existence of such a treaty is a testament to the fact that pre-existing grain circulation policies of the countries at that time tended to threaten the grain security of particular countries. The treaty acknowledged that "E'Di" could cause a serious problem, and that the grain shortage was recognized as a humanitarian crisis. The treaty made it clear that all countries recognized that disaster relief was shared responsibility.

Qing Di Each vassal state safeguarded the interests of grain-poor states through the "Wu E'Di Treaty". When the weather was favorable, grain-rich countries adopted the "Qing Di" policy, which encouraged grain exports to grain-poor states so as to create a fair distribution of grain.

这个盟约的建立，一是表明当时各国的粮食流通政策，在特定情况下可能危及列国的粮食安全；二是表明当时各国"遏籴"（禁止粮食出境）的现象相当严重；三是表明列国已认识到粮食缺乏是一种人道主义危机，救灾是大家共同的责任，不应受国界限制。

请籴 诸侯各国通过"毋遏籴盟约"维护了缺粮国的利益。当风调雨顺时，粮食剩余国则要通过"请籴"政策，鼓励粮食出口，促进粮食贸易，以调节诸侯国之间的粮食余缺。

但也出现过例外。春秋时期晋惠公五年（公元前646年），秦国发生饥荒，"请籴"于晋。晋国大夫庆郑认为，以前晋国遇到饥荒，秦国曾慷慨支援，如今秦国发生了饥荒，晋国理当还报。但是这个建议遭到惠公之舅虢射的反对，结果晋惠公采纳了虢射的意见，"不予秦粟"。由此可见，春秋时期，各国的粮食由国家统制管理，民间是不能自由开展粮食进出口贸易的。

此后，历朝都在借鉴前人的基础上，推行了一系列维护国计民生的粮食流通政策法规，有取有舍、扬抑结合，兴利除弊、安邦益民，使粮食流通的国家行为不断完善成熟，平衡了当时内政外交的各方利益，顺应了历史发展潮流。

二、粮食贸易属性

封建社会，国家征收的农业税以粮食实物税为主，因此粮食的生产经营是治国安邦的要务之一。粮食不仅是人们生产生活的主要物资，还是国家安全的重要战略物资、军需物资和工商业的重要资源。因而，粮食在其本质的自然属性以外，还附加着诸多社会属性，担当着类似货币和稀缺物资等的功能。

On a rare occasion, during the Spring and Autumn period of the 5th year of the reign of Prince Hui of Jin state (646 BC), Qin state asked for Jin for aid because a famine had hit. Qingzheng, an official of Jin state, held that, when Jin was in a famine state in the past, the state of Qin generously donated Jin. Many believed that the state of Jin should reciprocate. However, the return of the favor was proposal opposed by Guo She, Prince Hui's uncle. And Prince Hui accepted his uncle's counsel, and no donation was provided. This episode demonstrates that during the Spring and Autumn period, trade was under the strict control of the state. The private person could not trade grain freely.

From the time of the treaty, subsequent dynasties carried forward the lesson of their predecessors to implement grain circulation policies and regulations to safeguard equitable grain circulation and therefore protected the health of the national economy and people's livelihoods. At that time, the interests of all parties in internal affairs and diplomacy were closely linked to the grain trade.

II. The Nature of Grain Trade

In feudal society, the state-levied agricultural tax was actually payable in grain, and so it is clear that the production and management of grain was an important guarantee of the nation's peace and prosperity. Grain is not only key agriculture product and source of people's sustenance, but also an important resource for national security, military supplies, industry and commerce. It is for these reasons that grain can be understood to transcend a mere practical value, also functioned as a currency and a limited commodity.

1. 交换功能

产生于原始社会母系氏族兴盛时期或父系氏族开始时期的原始商品交易，就是粮食交易。传说神农氏领导的部落以农业为生，在有了一定的粮食剩余后，便开始了粮食与陶器或其他物品的交换活动。所谓"庖牺氏没，神农氏作，列廛于国，日中为市，致天下之民，聚天下之货，交易而退，各得其所"，指的就是粮食与其他物品的交易。这种粮物交换形式起源久远，持续了很长的历史阶段。

2. 支付功能

秦始皇灭六国后，统一了度量衡，《淮南子·主术训》记述："衡之于左右，无私轻重，故可以为平。"顾炎武在《郡县论七》中评论："量其冲僻，衡其繁简。"秦汉时期以"石"来计算粮食数量，官员的报酬"禄"以粮食计量支付。当时设置的一种官职就称为"二千石曹尚书"，"曹"为官署或衙门，"尚书"是官职。这些官员的俸禄为每年二千石谷。后来出现的"食禄阶层""吃皇粮"等说法，皆源于此。唐代白居易《观刈麦》的诗中"吏禄三百石，岁晏有余粮"，描述的就是朝廷对官员以粮付酬的情况。无论秦汉魏晋南北朝的"秩石制"，还是隋唐宋元明清的"禄米制"，都是严格按照官吏或军士的职务级别确定相应的俸禄标准，以"石"为单位，用粮食实物支付。新中国成立初期，国家在机关和军队实行供给制，以小米折价，用以支付干部军人的薪酬。

1. Function of Exchange

The primitive commodity trade began with grain in the days of matrilineal clan just before the development of patrilineal clan. In Chinese mythology, Shen Nong led a tribe of farmers, who after growing an abundance of grain began to exchange their harvest for pottery and other items. Chinese mythology relates that "after Paoxi (namely, Fuxi; credited with creating humanity in Chinese mythology) died, the Shennong's thrived, setting up a bazaar and allowing people to trade commodities during the daytime. The bazaar attracted people and gathered goods from different places to be traded". The trading mentioned in the legend refers to the exchange of grain for other goods. It was one of the earliest forms of exchange and lasted for a long period of Chinese history.

2. Function of Payment

After conquering six states, Emperor Qin Shihuang standardized the weights and measures across the nation. As is described in *Zhushuxun · Huainanzi*: "Carefully observing people and appointing impartially can be considered fair." As Gu Yanwu commented in *The Part Seven of the County Theory*: "It is better to compare the major and minor, and measure the complex and simple." In the Qin and Han dynasties, "*dan* (equivalent to 60 kilograms)" was a unit of measurement used to calculate the amount of grain. Remuneration for officials called "*lu*" was paid with the measurement of grain. At that time, there was an official position called "Cao Shangshu with two thousand *dan*", of which "Cao" referred to "*guanshu*" or "*yamen*" meaning the government, and "Shangshu" referred to a kind of official position. The salary of 2,000 *dan* was the basis of expressions such as "salaried class" and "grains granted from the emperor". Bai Juyi's (a well-known poet in Tang dynasty) poem of "Watching the Reapers" describes how the officials of the court were paid in grains: "Being granted 300 *dan* in salaries each year, with surplus grain reserved at the end of the year." Both the "Dan Measurement System" of Qin, Han, Wei, Jin and the Southern and Northern dynasties and the "Grain Salary System" of Sui, Tang, Song, Yuan, Ming and Qing dynasties were all strictly determined by the rank of officials or military personnel, all of whom were paid with grains by the "*dan*". In the early days of People's Republic of China, provisions system was implemented among the government agencies whereby cadres' and soldiers' salaries were paid in the form of grain discounts.

古代集市
The Ancient Market

3. 计价功能

历史上，如遭遇粮食运输困难或时局动乱的情况，官府也会将部分作为俸禄的谷粮等值折算为钱币发放给官员，或者采取"半钱半谷"的俸禄方式。明代永乐八年（公元1410年）就出现过朝廷令税粮课税俱折收钞的情形。同时，在交易市场上也存在以粮代钱，购换其他物资的现象。这种情况下，粮食充当着货币的一般等价物的角色。

4. 储备功能

中国历代统治者都将粮食储备视为国家安全的要政，提出了建立健全粮食储备、保障粮食安全的一系列政策主张和法律法规。通过流通渠道，集中收购调运，大力积蓄粮食，增强国家实力。《管子·牧民》开篇就讲："凡有地牧民者，务在四时，守在仓廪。国多财则远者来，地辟举则民留处。仓廪实则知礼节，衣食足则知荣辱。"

"手中有粮，心中不慌。"充裕的粮食是保障军需民生、保障经济社

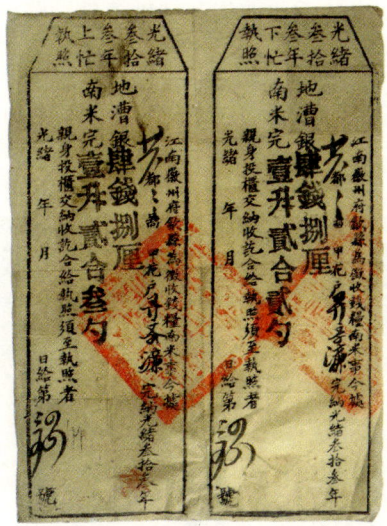

钱粮执照（光绪）·中国粮食博物馆藏
The License of Monetary and Grain (Guangxu) ·
Collected by Chinese Grain Museum

3. Function of Pricing

Historically, even in circumstances of difficulties facing grain transportation unrest, the government would convert part grain into coins to pay the officials, or pay half of their remuneration in grain and half in coins. In the eighth year of Yongle period of the Ming dynasty (1410 AD), the government would accept grain substitute for a portion of cash tax contributions. Similarly, the practice of exchanging grain for money began to appear in the marketplace. It can be seen from such phenomena that how grain was used as a kind of currency.

4. Function of Reserve

China's former dynastic rulers regarded grain reserves as priority of national security, and put forward a series of policies, propositions, laws and regulations for establishing and improving grain reserves and guaranteeing grain security. Through the circulation channels, ancient governments purchased and distributed grains collectively, accumulating massive amounts of grain to strengthen the nations they ruled over. *Herdsmen·Guanzi* opens with "any country that has land to feed people must farm in the best agricultural season for abundant grain

会发展、保障国家安全的重要前提和基础条件。藏粮于民就是老百姓积攒粮食，备战备荒，规避民乱国殇的风险。在国家层面就是统筹全局，保障粮食流通渠道通畅，预防各种不测，增强抵御自然风险、市场风险、军事风险、政治风险的能力。

丰图义仓（光绪）
Fengtu Yi (Public) Granary (Guangxu)

丰图义仓内院
Fengtu Yi (Public) Granary Cortile

granary. The country with rich financial resources attracts people from afar to settle down, and the land universally cultivated affords its people peace and security. If there is enough grain, people will become polite. It is only when grain and clothing are plentiful that people can understand the nature of honor and disgrace".

"With grain in hands, no panic in heart." Having enough grain is an important prerequisite and basic condition for supporting an army and safeguarding people's livelihood, economic and social development, and national security. "Storing grain for people" means that the people will have enough grain in times of famine, thereby preventing the civil chaos and national disaster. Ensuring the grain security, preventing varieties of emergencies, and resisting the risks of nature, market, military, and politics were the essence of national governance.

郧县大丰仓（明代）
Yunxian Dafeng Granary (Ming dynasty)

三、古代粮食运输

粮食的流通与贸易实现了其在不同范围间的空间位移，延展放大了其自身的经济社会属性。这种移动成行靠的是人工辗转腾挪和各式各样工具设备的运输。最早的粮食搬运方式是人们手提肩扛，后来发明了扁担挑运，随着车船的发明和畜力（牛、马、骆驼等）的驯养役使，粮食运输发生了历史性的变化，省时省力，运量增大，效率大为提高。

粮印（清代）• 中国粮食博物馆藏
Grain Printing (Qing Dynasty) • Collected by Chinese Grain Museum

运粮单印版（明代）• 中国粮食博物馆藏
Printing of Grain Transport Documents (Ming Dynasty) • Collected by Chinese Grain Museum

III. Grain Transportation in Ancient Times

The circulation and trade of grain were of great significance to the functioning of the economy and society. The movement of grain relied on people and various forms of transportation and tools. The earliest method of grain transportation came in the form of people carrying it on their shoulders. Before long, the carrying pole was invented. With the invention of carts and ships as well as the domestication of animal power (such as cattle, horses, camels, etc.), grain transportation underwent significant changes which meant that a great deal of time and energy could be saved. In addition, the capacity and efficiency of transportation was much increased.

运粮单据印版（明代）· 中国粮食博物馆
Printing of Grain Transport Documents (Ming Dynasty) ·
Collected by Chinese Grain Museum

1. 人背肩挑

在生产力落后的远古时代，人们转运粮食的主要形式就是手提、肩扛、背负、担挑等，体力消耗大，搬运数量少，工作效率低，耗费时间长。

条篮·中国粮食博物馆藏
Bamboo Basket · Collected by Chinese Grain Museum

扁担·中国粮食博物馆藏
Shoulder Pole · Collected by Chinese Grain Museum

2. 牲畜驮运

新石器时代晚期，人们开始驯养大型草食动物，如马、牛、象、驼、驴等，役使其驮运挽车，粮食运输由此进入了生产力提高的新阶段。畜力运粮负载能力强，运距可长可短，在崎岖不便的道路上长途跋涉也履险如夷，是农业文明史上的一大亮点。

1. Labor Transportation

The primitive nature of grain production is reflected by the ways in which grain was transported. Grain was typically carried by hand, on the shoulder, back and by shoulder pole. Such a method of transportation was physically exhausting and little grain could be moved in this way. It was inefficient and time consuming.

木篓·中国粮食博物馆藏
Wood Basket · Collected by Chinese Grain Museum

2. Livestock Transportation

In the late Neolithic period, large herbivores such as horse, cattle, elephant, camel, donkey were domesticated and used for transporting goods and cart pulling. So it was that grain transportation entered a new stage of productivity. Despite the long transportation distances and uneven roads, animal-powered grain transport capacity was reliable. The livestock transportation represented a turning point in the development of grain transport.

驮篓 · 中国粮食博物馆藏
Pack Basket · Collected by Chinese Grain Museum

3. 车具运输

车是一项重要发明。考古发掘表明，中国在商代晚期已使用双轮马车，而在此前，独轮手推车就已经发明并投入使用。手推、畜拉车具的应用使粮食运输方式得到进一步改善，运输效率得到进一步提高，为推动经济社会的发达进步做出了很大贡献。

独轮车 · 中国粮食博物馆藏
Wheelbarrow · Collected by Chinese Grain Museum

4. 舟船驳运

受落后交通工具的运能所限，古时有民谚说"百里不贩薪，千里不籴粮"，意思是远距离买粮运输成本太大很不划算。但是，在水路船运业发达以后，这种观念就被彻底颠覆了。人们借助水路网络，把粮食运

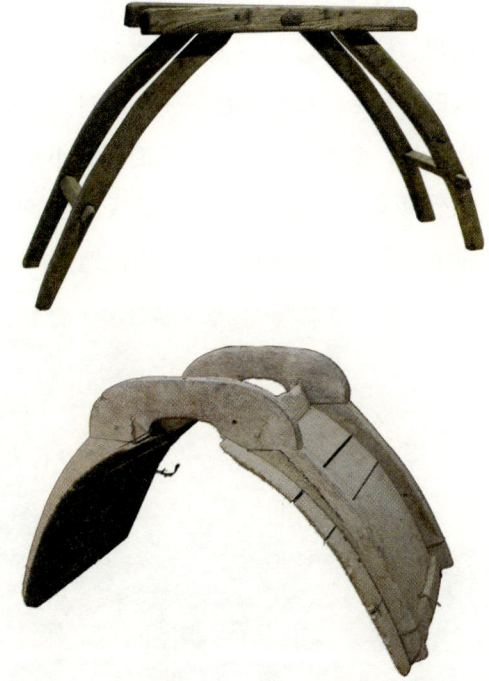

驮架·中国粮食博物馆藏
Pack Frame · Collected by Chinese Grain Museum

3. Vehicle Transportation

The advent of carriage is an important point in Chinese history. Archaeological excavations have shown that two-wheeled carriages were used in China in the late Shang dynasty, and wheelbarrows had been invented sometime before. The application of hand-push and animal-pull vehicles meant more efficient grain transportation, and drove forward the development of the economy and society.

4. Shipment Transportation

It was because of the limitations of primitive means of transportation that the expression "No selling wood further a hundred miles, and no selling grain further

往各地进行贸易,经济效益显著,再也没有成本过高、得不偿失的困惑了。宋元之际,扬州、杭州、苏州三大城市之间的粮食商贸活动十分活跃,史书记载:"江湖连接,无地不通,一舟出门,万里惟意,靡有碍隔。民计每岁种食之外,余米尽以贸易。大商则聚小家之所有,小舟亦附大舰而同营,展转贩粜,以规厚利。"舟船贩运物畅其流,进入流通领域的粮食,按照市场导向和官方计划,成规模地走得更远。

漕运码头·山东博物馆
Water Transportation Wharf · Shandong Museum

than a thousand" came into being. The cost of long-distance grain transportation was too high and uneconomical. However, the saying was turned upside down with the advances of the waterway shipping industry. People utilized the waterway network to ship grain to various places for trading. With elimination of excessive costs and losses, the economic benefits were undeniable. During the Song and Yuan dynasties, the grain trade between the three major cities of Yangzhou, Hangzhou and Suzhou was flourishing. Historical records: "The all-round transportation connecting rivers and lakes helps people to reach anywhere. One ship can solve all the transportation problems. Surplus grain can be traded in the market after self-sufficient food storage. Many farmers' surplus rice was first purchased by the small merchants, then by the big merchants. They would then transport the grain to cities and remote markets for huge profits."

运粮船·山东博物馆
Victualer · Shandong Museum

第三章

漕运春秋

Chapter 3

History of Water Transportation

漕运是中国历史上一项重要的经济制度。所谓漕运,就是利用水道调运公粮的专业运输,历代将其视为"岁贡之命脉"。彼时,朝廷将征集的田赋粮食,由水路解往京师或军政市镇,以供宫廷消费、百官俸禄、兵士军饷和民食调剂。在平常的语境中,漕运仅指通过运河或者沟通运河的天然河道转运粮食的经济活动。

漕运的通渠积谷功能推进了南北方经济文化交流和国家兴盛统一。历代多少旷世英雄,纵横捭阖安抚天下,文功武治,实现雄图霸业,漕运之力,功不可没。

漕运码头场景
Scene of Caoyun Boats at the Dock

一、跌宕兴衰

漕运在粮食流通和南北交通方面发挥了突出作用。公元前 647 年,周襄王五年,晋灾荒,借粮于秦,粮船由水道从雍至晋都绛,史称"泛舟之役",为中国大规模漕运之始。公元前 486 年,吴王夫差筑邗城,

Water transportation (hereafter referred to as "caoyun"), renowned for being the waterway dedicated to grain transportation, is an important part of China's economic infrastructure and regarded as the lifeline for annual dynastic tributes. In ancient China, the collected tax grain was transported through waterways by the government to the capital or to military cities or towns for the purpose of royal consumption, officials salaries, soldiers' pay and provision, as part of the food supply of the common people. Caoyun can be understood as the transportation of grain via canals or rivers.

Caoyun, which involved the digging of channels and grain storage, promoted economic and cultural exchange between the north and the south, and brought about the unification and prosperity for the whole nation. Caoyun made an indispensable contribution to successful governance on the part of various distinguished dynastic heroes.

Ⅰ. Rise and Decline

Caoyun played an outstanding role in grain logistics and transportation between the north and the south. In 647 BC, the 5th year of the reign of King Xiang of Zhou dynasty, the state of Jin borrowed grain from the state of Qin because Jin was suffering from a famine. Grain boats departed from Yong city of Qin to Jiang city, the capital of Jin via the waterways. The event recorded in history as the "Boating Campaign" is thought to represent the beginning of caoyun. In 486 BC, King Fuchai of Wu State built up Han city and canalized Hangou to connect the Yangtze River and Huaihe River in order to conquer the north. This was an essential precursor to the construction of the building of the Big Canal from the north to south. In the 3rd century BC, the First Emperor of Qin transported military grain provision from Shandong to Beihe (around Wujiahe River in Inner Mongolia) to support his attack on the Xiongnu. In his subsequent campaign against Nanyue State (Guangdong province and Guangxi province), the Lingqu Canal was built to transport military grain provision to guarantee triumph. Caoyun continued to play decisive roles in the fate of the nation and each dynasty attached great importance to it.

开凿邗沟,连通江、淮二水,以图北方,此举成为开凿南北大运河的首功。公元前200多年秦始皇攻打匈奴,部署了将山东粮食通过水道运往北河(内蒙古乌加河一带)以充军粮的军事行动。之后,秦军征战南越(两广地区),凿通灵渠,运送粮饷,充实军需给养,保证了战事胜局。漕运由此发展,彰显其在国运兴衰中举足轻重的作用,受到历代重视。

  灵渠 灵渠又称湘桂运河、兴安运河,在广西兴安县境内,于秦始皇三十三年(公元前214年)由秦将史禄率军民劈山削崖,艰苦开凿而成,全长37公里。灵渠将湘江水三七分流,其中三分水向南流入漓江,七分水向北汇入湘江,联结湘江和漓江,沟通了长江、珠江两大水系,

灵渠鸟瞰图
Bird's-eye View of the Lingqu Canal

The Lingqu Canal　Also known as the Xianggui Canal, or the Xing'an Canal, the Lingqu Canal is 37 km long. It was built in the 33rd year of Emperor Qin Shi Huang (214 BC) by soldiers and civilians under the leadership of Shi Lu, a General of Qin State. Lingqu Canal connects the Lijiang and Xiangjiang rivers. This was done by diverting 30% of the Xianjiang's current into the southward flowing Lijiang river. The remaining 70% flows northward into the Yangtze River and Zhujiang River Systems. This split enabled the transportation of reinforcements and provisions to the front. It played a crucial role in the First Emperor of Qin's conquests of the central plains, and was regarded as a strategic passage between the Three Chu (West Chu, East Chu and South Chu) and the Two Yue (Nan Yue and Min Yue) regions. In 1058 AD, during the Renzong period of the Song dynasty, the Lingqu Canal was extended to ensure a strong transport network. Following the appearance of the railway and the development of road transport, the land transportation evolved, the Lingqu Canal began to play a greater role in irrigation, and less in transportation. After the founding of the People's Republic of China, branch canals and reservoirs were built along the Lingqu Canal which played an active role ensuring a high grain yield and a peaceful existence for the nation's people. The Lingqu Canal is one of China's key cultural preservation units.

　　In the Western Han dynasty, grain waterway transportation extended all over the country supplying the capital via the Yellow River and the Weishui River. In 129 AD, Liu Che, Emperor Wu of the Han dynasty developed canal building and waterway transportation. Grain was transported from areas east of Hanguguan Gate via a route over 150 km long of Yellow River, which efficiently shortened the caoyun shipping time from Tongguan to Chang'an, and helped to irrigate about 67,000 hectares of farmland. Large, strong boats were a good choice when it came to transporting grain along the swift, turbulent Yellow River, but they were unsuitable for the shallow and sandy waters of the Weishui River. Therefore, a large-scale Jingshi granary was built at the intersection of the Yellow River and Weishui River for unloading grain and transferring it on to smaller flat-bottomed boats. In *Ping zhun book · Records of the Historian*, it is recorded that several hundred thousand *dan* of grain was transported east to Yaoshan Mountain by means of caoyun and land transportation to supply the officials in the capital each

便于把军事援兵和粮食补给运往前线，为秦始皇最终把这一带广大地区划入中原王朝的版图、经略岭南、完成统一大业发挥了重要作用，一向被视为"三楚两粤之咽喉"。公元1058年，宋仁宗时期继续修凿灵渠，保证水运畅通。近代因铁路、公路的修筑，陆路交通逐渐发达，灵渠通航作用逐渐消失，遂成以灌溉为主的河渠。新中国成立后，灵渠沿岸新建了许多水渠、水库等，为当地粮丰民安继续发挥着重要作用。灵渠现在是中国重点文物保护单位。

西汉建都长安，"河渭漕挽天下，西给京师"。公元前129年，武帝刘彻大兴漕运，开凿漕渠，利用黄河的一段长约三百里的航道，从函谷关以东各地向关中漕运粮食，使潼关到长安水路运输的路程和时间大大缩短，并溉田万余顷。因黄河水急浪大，漕船多为坚固的大型木船，不能进入水浅沙深的渭水和狭窄的人工漕渠到达京都长安，所以专门修建了规模很大的京师仓，用于卸粮中转，以便在渭水入黄处换用平底小船继续漕运。《史记·平准书》记载："漕转山东粟，以给中都官，岁不过数十万石。"此时，漕运已逐渐制度化。

魏晋南北朝时期，为运输军粮和各种物资，南北各地先后修缮疏浚了秦汉时期遗留的旧漕渠，并因地制宜地开凿了许多新漕渠，形成地跨南北、沟通河海的漕运网。

隋初，文帝在长安建都，重振渭水漕运，兴盛一时。开皇三年（公元583年），朝廷下诏在蒲、陕、虢、熊、伊、洛、郑、怀、邵、卫、汴、许、汝等临水十三州设置募水丁，漕运关东及汾晋等地谷粟以供应京师。隋炀帝即位后，利用天然河流和旧有渠道组织开凿通济渠，连接海河、黄河、淮河、长江和钱塘江五大水系，开通了以洛阳为中心，北到涿郡（今北京），南抵余杭的水上交通大动脉——隋唐大运河，形成了南北漕运新通道，为巩固国家统一、促进南北经济文化交流发挥了重大作用，影响深远。

唐高祖李渊定都长安后，粮食问题首当其冲。因为关中一带不足以

year. In the Han dynasty, caoyun was gradually institutionalized.

In the Wei-Jin and Southern and Northern dynasty, the old canals of the Qin and Han dynasties were repaired and dredged. The new canals were built according to local conditions for the transportation of military grain and provisions. A caoyun network extended from the south to the north, and connected the canals to sea.

At the beginning of the Sui dynasty, Emperor Wen founded the capital in Chang'an, and regenerated the caoyun system in the Weishui River, which then flourished. In the 3rd year of Emperor Kaihuang Reign (583 AD), the imperial government recruited waterway soldiers in 13 cities along rivers, i.e. Puzhou, Shanzhou, Huozhou, Xiongzhou, Yizhou, Luozhou, Zhengzhou, Huaizhou, Shao zhou, Weizhou, Bian zhou, Xuzhou and Ruzhou. Grain from east of Hangu Gate and Fenshui Basin in Shanxi province could be transported along the waterways to supply the capital. After the succession of Emperor Yang, making use of rivers and old canals, the Tongji Canal was built to connect 5 water systems of the Haihe River, the Yellow River, the Huaihe River, the Yangtze River and the Qiantang River. With the Great Canal of Sui and Tang Dynasty, the main artery of waterway communication was built. The Great Canal system had Luoyang its center and connected the north end of Zhuojun (modern Beijing) and the south end of Yuhang, a new channel of caoyun formed. The new canal system ensured the provision of enough grain for the imperial government and consolidated the status of the state, exerting a profound influence.

Following his settlement in Chang'an, grain became the most important issue for Kao Tsu of the Tang dynasty's Li Yuan period. This was due to the fact that there were stark shortages in the supply of grain in the Guanzhong region of the Shaanxi plain which meant that there was not enough grain to provide for the large population living in the capital Chang'an. Therefore, there was an urgent need to bring in grain from other cities. Although a number of measures were taken to tackle the issue of grain shortages, none of them would prove effective in the long term. It was for this reason that during the Xuanzong period of the Tang dynasty, great efforts were made to consolidate water transportation (caoyun). At the time, cargo ships encountered difficulties when entering into the Wei River due sediment buildup and shallow waters. In order to counter these challenges,

供给首都庞大规模人口的粮食需求，亟待从外地输入，以解短缺之困。于是采取各种措施，消解缺粮难题，但都是只能应急，难以持久。到了唐玄宗时期，决定大力整顿漕运。当时渭水淤沙水浅，漕船难进，宰相裴耀卿"条上漕事便宜"，提出"节级转运法"，以重建关中漕运事业。规划将漕程分设三段：洛口以东为水运，置河口仓，东南漕舟至此输粟入仓；另换船装运分入河、洛，至三门峡东西两侧登岸；凿山路18里陆运，以避三门之险。从而健全了漕运各个环节，提高了运粮效率。到天宝年间，每年运往长安的漕粮高达四百万石，可以供养一百万人，足够大唐政府运转之用，长安崇高的帝都地位得到巩固。

"安史之乱"将唐政府经济支柱之一的黄河流域荡为烽火战场。后战乱平息，但河北藩镇割据，成为动乱的策源地，朝廷不得不更多地依赖江淮流域经济区，"兵食所资在东南"。运输东南粮物，漕运尤为关键。故在唐代宗广德二年（公元764年），刘晏接手改革漕运，疏浚水道，训练漕卒，制造坚船，减少了损耗，降低了费用，提高了漕运效率。晚唐历史就是一部运河争夺史，能控制运河，保持住漕运，帝国就能幸存，否则便会土崩瓦解。

北宋定都汴梁（开封），坐享黄河之利，当地粮丰廪实，朝野暂无须漕运兴作。到公元972年，宋太祖开宝五年，始改革江淮漕运。公元1019年，宋真宗天禧三年，开扬州"古河"，疏通漕运。

元代贯通了京杭大运河，漕运鼎盛时，8000多艘河运漕船南来北往，川流不息地把江南漕粮运到大都（今北京）积水潭码头，每年达四五百万石之巨。作为大运河北端的终点站，北京什刹海附近的烟袋斜街、钟鼓楼一带，商贾云集，歌台酒榭，湖光水色，成为元大都一处最繁华的所在。

明代建国后，初期定都南京，无须漕运，北京什刹海盛况不再，渐渐萧条荒废。后明成祖朱棣迁都北京，无暇整治漕运，渡口遂退至通州，所运粮货转陆运至北京。明神宗时期，张居正推行改革，任用专家

prime minister Pei Yaoqing proposed a method of gradual transportation to the imperial court. Water transportation would be divided into three stages. The first stage saw cargo ships, which originated in the southeast transporting their grain to Hekou granary via the river to the east of Luokou. The second stage was to transfer the grain onto other ships going to Hekou and Luokou, and unload it on the east and south sides of Sanmen Gorge. The final stage was to dig roads on mountains, each around 18 *li* in length, for land-transportation in order to avoid the difficulties presented by traversing the Sanmen Gorge. On their completion, the different stages of caoyun represented much greater efficiency for grain transportation. By the Tianbao period of the Tang dynasty, the total volume of grain being transported to Chang'an had risen to 4 million *dan*. This was enough to provide for 1 million people each year. This achievement consolidated the Tang dynasty's imperial status.

The Rebellion of An Lushan and Shi Siming saw the Yellow River drainage area, the pillar of the national economy, consumed by the fires of war. The area to the North of the river became a hotbed for rebellions due to the military governorship that called the area home. The imperial government had no choice but to rely more on the economic zones of the Yangtze-Huaihe drainage area. Military grain and provisions came from southeast, and caoyun became very important for the transportation. Therefore, in the 2nd year (764 AD) of Guangde Regime of Daizong, Liu Yan took over the reform of caoyun. He dredged the channel, trained waterway solders and built solid boats — the move, which reduced loss, decreased costs and improved the efficiency of caoyun transport. The history of the late Tang dynasty is history of battles for control on the canal. If an empire is able to control the canal and maintain the caoyun system, it will prosper, if not, it will fall apart.

Bianliang (modern day Kaifeng) was chosen for the site of the capital during the North Song dynasty. Taking the advantages of the Yellow River for ample grain, the imperial government did not have to revitalize caoyun. In the 5th year of Kaibao Regime of Emperor Taizu (972 AD), the caoyun of the Yangtze River and Huaihe River was reformed. In 1019 AD, the 3rd year of Tianxi Regime of Emperor Zhenzong, the Old Canal of Yangzhou was dredged so it could become a part of the caoyun system.

治理黄河，使黄、淮二河分流入海，南北运河恢复通航。

京杭大运河
The Grand Canal of Beijing-Hangzhou

清康熙时期，大力修治黄河，任命专职官员（河道总督），重用水利专家，组织大量民工，耗时十年，终使"黄河故道，次第修复，而漕运大通"。咸丰五年（公元 1855 年）黄河改道致运河浅梗，水路不畅，漕运的地位日渐衰落。后随着政经形势的变化，光绪二十七年（1901年），清政府下令停止漕运。至光绪三十一年（1905 年），因河运已废，故裁撤了漕运管理机构。辛亥革命后，漕运制度废除。

二、转漕、漕辇与中转粮仓

漕运过程中有两个重要环节："转漕"与"漕辇"，就是漕粮运输形式和工具的转接与变化。转漕，车运称"转"，水运称"漕"，即先把产地的官粮用车辆运到附近的河道码头，然后装入漕船运往目的地；漕辇，就是先水路后陆路，把粮食由漕船运至码头后，转上陆路车辆，送达目的地。陆路和水路的承接转换，形成了相互配套、前后衔接的序列

In the Yuan dynasty, the Beijing-Hangzhou Grand Canal was dredged. In the heyday of the caoyun network, there were over 8,000 boats shuttling back and forth to transport grain with the annual loads of grain up to 4 to 5 million *dan* from the regions south of the Yangtze River to the Jishuitan Wharf in Dadu (modern day Beijing). The Yandai Xie Street and the Bell & Drum Tower surrounding the Shicha Lake of Beijing with picturesque sceneries, as the terminal of north of the Grand Canal, was regarded the most prosperous place of the Great Capital of the Yuan dynasty, in a hustle and bustle picture.

Nanjing became the seat of the capital in the early stages of the Ming dynasty, and the no longer flourishing Shicha Lake of Beijing was gradually abandoned. Later, the third emperor of the Ming dynasty, Ming Chengzu, moved the capital to Beijing. As he was too busy to regulate the grain transport system, the ferry port was moved to Tongzhou, and grain was transferred to Beijing by land. During the reign of emperor Shenzong of the Ming dynasty, Zhang Juzheng carried out reform and appointed experts to govern the Yellow River. The Yellow River and Huaihe River were channeled into the sea, and the north-south canal was restored for navigation.

During the Kangxi period of the Qing dynasty, the Yellow River was vigorously repaired. Full-time officials (river governors) were appointed, water conservancy experts were reemployed, and a large number of migrant workers were enlisted in the work. After a long period of ten years, "the old road of the Yellow River was repaired, and the canal transport became larger". In the fifth year of Xianfeng (1855 AD), the diversion of the Yellow River caused the canal to become shallow and unnavigable. Later, after political and economic change, the Qing government ordered the cessation of grain transportation in 1901 AD. In the thirty-first year of Guangxu dynasty (1905 AD), the canal transport administration was abolished because of the disuse of the river transport system. After the Revolution of 1911, the grain transport system was abolished.

II. Land-to-water Transportation, Water-to-land Transportation and Grain Transfer Granary

There are two important processes in the workings of caoyun, namely land-

化漕运作业流程。

漕运图
A Picture of Caoyun

唐代称漕辇为纲运，"船每以十艘为一纲，载江南谷麦，自淮泗入汴，抵河阳，每船一千石"。之后的朝代，漕辇在货运种类、线路和管理等方面都有了较大的变化，但其水运的形式和功能经久不衰。

为保障漕运粮食安全，历朝历代在漕运的每个重要节点都兴建了规模不同的粮食中转仓库。

敖仓 秦朝实施漕运，当时最主要的问题就是运东方的粮食以实咸阳，从全局来看，最重要的转运中心在中原，因此秦政府建中国最大的粮仓——敖仓于成皋（在今河南省荥阳市）。这个粮仓已经有物流中心的影子，开始实行统一配送了。在楚汉争霸之时，敖仓常常成为双方争夺的目标，这个粮仓对战争的进程产生着深刻的影响。刘邦先下手为

to-water transportation and water-to-land transportation. The two differ in terms of their respective modes of transport, and the tools use therein. Land-to-water transportation combined both water-way and land-way transportation. Official grain was first transported from the field to the nearest wharf, and then to its final destination via the canals. Water-to-land transportation implied that the first part of the grain's journey would be river bound, and the second part would involve carts of the land. Together, the two kinds of transport constituted a complete and connected operation.

Water-to-land transportation was called Gang Transportation in the Tang dynasty. Gang is a flotilla consisting of 10 boats. Each boat was loaded 1,000 *dan* of grain from Jiangnan and arrived at Heyang via the Sishui River, Huaihe River and Bianshui River. During subsequent dynasties, great changes took place in the methods of freight, in the routes the way transport was managed, but the form and function of water transportation remained unchanged.

In order to ensure grain security through the caoyun process, grain transit warehouses of different sizes were built at each important node of caoyun throughout successive dynasties.

Ao Granary　The great challenge which caoyun faced in the Qin dynasty was the issue of transporting grain from the East to Xianyang. The most important transit hub was in the Central Plains. Therefore, the imperial government of the Qin dynasty built the largest granary in China—Ao granary in Chenggao (present Xingyang, Henan province). It functioned as the primary logistic center and was a means of unified distribution. During the Chu-Han War, Ao granary was often regarded as the target for both belligerents, and so it is easy to see how the granary had a profound impact on the course of the war. Liu Bang took the first strike. "He stationed Xingyang with troops and built a military road to the Yellow River for transporting the grain from Ao granary." Later it would be captured by King Xiang several times. Afraid of grain shortage and forced to sue for peace, the emperor of Han ceded the territory west of Xingyang.

The importance of Ao granary in the war is clearly recorded in *The Records of the Grand Historian*. After it was decided that Chang'an would be the location of the capital of the Western Han dynasty, a large amount of grain was transported from the east to Hangu Gate every year. Ao granary continuously

强,"军荥阳,筑甬道,属之河,以取敖仓粟"。但随后"项王数侵夺汉甬道,汉王食乏,恐,请和,割荥阳以西为汉"。

《史记》的记载清晰地表明了敖仓在那场战争中的重要性。西汉定都长安后,每年也需从关东运输大量谷物,在当时的漕运网络中,敖仓仍很重要。汉武帝宠幸的王夫人,曾请求将其子封到洛阳为王,被汉武帝坚决拒绝,理由就是"洛阳有武库、敖仓,当关口,天下咽喉,自先帝以来,传不为置王"。

黎阳仓 黎阳仓位于卫州黎阳县(今河南浚县)西南,建立于隋文帝时期,一直沿用至北宋,时间长达600多年。黎阳仓西濒永济渠,东临黄河,依托隋唐大运河水运便利,是具有中转性质的粮仓。隋唐时期都在此置军镇守督运漕粮,是重要国仓之一,被誉为"天下名仓"。

黎阳仓
Liyang Granary

played an vital role in the caoyun network at that time. Emperor Wu's favorite wife, Princess Wang once requested the Emperor to grant her son the title of King in Luoyang, but the Emperor firmly refused, saying that "there are military arsenals and Ao granary in Luoyang, which serve as the gateway and throat of the empire. Since the times of the first emperor, Luoyang has never had a king".

Liyang Granary Located in the southwest of Liyang county, Weizhou (present Xunxian county, Henan province), Liyang granary was established in the reign of Emperor Wen of the Sui dynasty and was used until the Northern Song dynasty, meaning it operated for a period of more than 600 years. Liyang granary is close to Yongji Canal in the west, and to its east lies the Yellow River. Relying on the Grand Canal of Sui-Tang dynasties, its operation is determined by its role as a transit granary. During the Sui and Tang dynasties, military towns were set up to guard grain cargo. Liyang granary was often referred to as the most famous grain granary in the kingdom.

Luokou Granary Luokou granary was also known as Xingluo granary. Soon after ascended the throne in 605 AD, Emperor Yang of the Sui dynasty issued an imperial edict to set Luoyang as the capital before he went on to dig the Grand Canal. The Grand Canal was built from Luoyang to the Yellow River via the Luohe River. It was then built along two routes, one of which reached Yuhang (today's Hangzhou) in the south and the other led to Zhuozhou (today's Beijing) in the north. As the Grand Canal was beginning to take shape, Luokou became the hub of this huge water transportation network.

In the second year of Daye (606 AD) in Sui dynasty, Luokou granary was built in the southeast of Gong county (today's Gongyi, Henan province) to store the grain transported from the South of the Yangtze River through the Grand Canal.

After the completion of the Grand Canal, which was over 2,000 kilometers long, the government of the Sui dynasty built many granaries at important nodes along the route, mainly for the transshipment of grain. Due to different and varying conditions at the different places along the route, the riverflow, sand content vary considerably. For this reason, it was impossible to reply on merely one kind of ship to complete the whole journey. Therefore, it is necessary that granaries should be built at various nodes along the canal to facilitate the

洛口仓 洛口仓也叫兴洛仓，公元605年，隋炀帝即位不久，就下令建都洛阳，同时下令开凿大运河。大运河以洛阳为起点，经洛河入黄河，然后分两路开凿，向南终点为余杭（今杭州），向北终点为涿州（今北京）。而在大运河初具雏形之时，人们不经意地发现，洛口成了这个庞大水运网的中枢。

因此，隋大业二年（606年），在巩县（今河南巩义）东南兴建洛口仓，把从江南经大运河运来的粮食囤积于此。

大运河完工后，隋王朝在沿线重要的节点设置了不少粮仓，主要用于中转漕粮。大运河长2000多公里，由于各地自然条件不同，不同河段的流量、含沙量以及河床特点各不相同，不可能依靠同一艘船一次运到，需要转换适合不同河段的船只和熟悉不同河段的水工分段运输。因此就需要在沿线节点兴建粮仓，以方便转运。如此一来，运河与粮仓形成了一个完整的漕运系统。而位于大运河庞大水运网三岔口的洛口，顿时有了举足轻重的地位。洛口仓筑有仓城，周围二十余里，"穿三千窖，每窖容八千石""置监官并镇兵千人守卫"。全仓储米约有二千四百万石，是隋朝最大的粮仓，也成为大运河最大、最重要的物流中心。

洛口仓如一座大容量的水库，各地的漕粮，通过庞大的水运网络，如水流般在这里蓄积；由此往西可运往洛阳、长安；而用兵东北时，又可由此运粮渡黄河，经永济渠而运往东北。

隋末天下大乱之时，这个粮仓更是成为影响天下大局的关键所在。谁拥有了天下第一粮仓，谁就有了争夺天下的资本。当时一度最有可能称霸中原、一统天下、赫赫有名的瓦岗军，就是在夺取洛口后迅速发展壮大起来，而在失洛口后又迅速崩溃的。李密夺取洛口仓时，洛口仓已兴建十一年，十一年储备的粮食，转眼间成了李密的盘中餐。有了洛口仓，瓦岗军发展堪称神速。大量的饥民加入，许多缺粮的义军陆续投奔，短短数月，瓦岗军达到鼎盛时期，改称他们为"洛口军"似乎也不为过。李密攻洛阳时，因为有洛口仓和回洛仓在手，洛阳已陷无粮境

unloading and reloading of grain onto the different ships. The canal and granaries formed a complete grain transport system, and Luokou, located at the fork of the Grand Canal's huge water transport network, played a pivotal role. The outer wall of Luokou granary was 10 kilometers long surrounding 3,000 underground granaries, each with a capacity of 8,000 *dan*. An inspector was appointed and 1,000 soldiers were stationed to keep guard. With 24 million *dan* of grain storage capacity, the granary was the largest one in the Sui dynasty, and served as the Grand Canal's largest and most important logistical hub.

Just as water retained in a large reservoir and fed by a huge water network, it was that grain from all over the country was stored in Luokou granary, arriving there by means of just such a huge water transport network. Grain stored at Luoko could be transported to Luoyang and Chang'an in the west. When the army was deployed in the northeast, grain could be transported across the Yellow River and moved to the northeast through the Yongji Canal.

Society fell into disorder and unrest at the end of the Sui dynasty, and so the nation's fate came to depend on the granary. Whoever controlled the largest granary controlled the kingdom. At that time, the Wagang Army, which was the most likely to dominate the central plains and unify the whole country had developed rapidly after seizing control of Luokou, but fell apart just as quickly after it lost control of Luokou. When Li Mi seized Luokou granary, it had already prospered for eleven years. Eleven years' worth of grain reserves fell right into his hands. With Luokou granary, the Wagang Army grew at a lightning speed. A large number of the starving masses enlisted, and many of the rebels suffering food shortages successively defected to join the Wagang Army. In just a few months, the Wagang Army reached peak strength. They might as well have been called the "Luokou Army". When Li Mi decided to attack Luoyang, the city was in of the throes of a grain shortage because both Luokou granary and Huiluo granary were then under his control. It might have been because he was blinded by his own victory streak in battle, or perhaps he underestimated Wang Shichong. Whatever the reason, Li Mi did not accept the strategy of waiting Luoyang run out of grain leading to the city's inevitable surrender. Impatient, Li Mi attacked and was quickly defeated, losing the precious Luokou granary. The loss of Luokou granary meant that the Wagang Army had lost its source of strength. The several

地。也许是因为前面的一连串胜利蒙蔽了他的双眼,也许是看不起王世充,李密没有听取手下围而不攻,等洛阳乏粮时不战而胜的策略,急于出战。最终一战而败,失去了洛口。失去洛口仓之后,瓦岗军没有了根基,数十万之众,一夜间崩溃。李密只好前去投奔李渊,后来又想叛逃,被李渊手下将领所杀。可以说,这位乱世英雄大起大落、大悲大喜的人生,都跟洛口仓有着牵扯不清的关系。正所谓,成也洛口,败也洛口。

后来李世民攻打洛阳,采取了跟李密前期一样的"攻略":先打下洛口仓,再打下回洛仓,使洛阳城陷入断粮的困境。不过李世民终不是李密,他再也没给王世充机会,围死洛阳后,最终令因饥饿失去抵抗力的王世充俯首称臣。

洛口仓复原图
Palinspastic Picture of Luokou Granary

还有隋唐建置的回洛仓、含嘉仓等也都可谓是隋唐大运河沿岸的重

hundred thousand strong force disintegrated overnight. Li Mi was forced to join Li Yuan. He was eventually killed by one of Li Yuan's general as he attempted to flee. Luokou granary was the energy behind the rise and fall, the sorrows and the joys of our hero Li Mi. For Li Mi, Luokou granary was water that bore the boat, and finally swallowed it.

Later, When Li Shimin attacked Luoyang, he adopted the same strategy as Li Mi. He captured Luokou granary first, and then Huiluo granary, which made Luoyang once again found itself caught in the jaws of a grain shortage. However, Li Shimin was different, and he never gave Wang Shichong a chance. After Li Shimin's siege of Luoyang, Wang Shichong, weakened by hunger would finally kneel before his new ruler.

Granaries which were operated during the Sui and Tang dynasties, such as Huiluo granary, Hanjia granary and others were important because they played the roles of transit granaries along the Sui and Tang Grand Canal.

Shuici Granary in the Ming Dynasty Shuici granaries, also known as Zhongzhuan, Zhuanyun, Zhuanshu, and Zhuanban granaries, were national grain reserve depots built along canals or natural rivers as part of the grain transit network. With the improvement of the management system, the granary would eventually bear the responsibility for supplying disaster relief grain, stabilizing grain prices, making up for caoyun grain deficits, and allocating grain for military supplies, and water conservancy projects.

In 1368 AD, Zhu Yuanzhang founded the Ming Empire with Nanjing as the capital. He then captured Dadu to the North, which he renamed Beiping Prefecture. In the first year of the Yongle period (1403 AD), Beiping was renamed as Beijing in anticipation of its promotion to the status of the nation's capital. In 1421 AD, the capital was officially moved to Beijing. From that point on a large amount of grain was transported from southeast China to the new capital via the canals. Since Huai'an, Xuzhou, Dezhou, Linqing, Tianjin and other places were easily accessible by waterway, the government built Shuici granaries with huge capacities in those places.

Fengji Granary in Huai'an Huai'an was an important port along the canal entering the Huaihe River, and also an important component within the caoyun for each dynasty. It was also the location of the "Office of the General

要中转粮仓。

明代的漕运水次仓 水次仓又叫中转仓、转运仓、转输仓、转搬仓，是为转运存储漕粮而在运河或自然河流沿岸设立的国家直属粮库。后随着管理制度的日臻完善，逐渐兼具赈灾、救济、平抑粮价、填补漕粮缺额、拨付军需用粮和水利工程用粮等功能。

1368 年，朱元璋建立明王朝并定都南京，遂北征攻占大都，改名北平府。永乐元年（1403 年）正月，升北平为北京。永乐十九年（1421 年）迁都北京。此后，东南地区的粮食由运河大量输入京师，由于淮安、徐州、德州、临清、天津等地水路畅达，便于漕粮汇集发运，因此当时政府在这些地方都建有仓容巨大的水次仓。

淮安的丰济仓 淮安是运河入淮的重要口岸，是历代漕运必经的咽喉要地，也是明朝中央设立的"漕运总督署"所在地，因而建在这里的丰济仓自然有着显耀的规模和地位。

丰济仓遗址
Relics of Fengji Granary

徐州广运仓 徐州是大运河的重要口岸，从河南东流的汴水和由东向南流的泗水交汇于此，是江淮通向中原的必经之地。明代时，每年经

Superintendent of Grain Transportation", which had been built up by the imperial government of the Ming dynasty. With such an important location, it is understandable why Fengji granary's status and physical scale was remarkable.

Guangyun Granary in Xuzhou Xuzhou is an important port along the Grand Canal, situated at the point where Bianshui River, which flows from the east of Henan province and meets Sishui River as it flows from the east southwards. During the Ming dynasty, more than 12,000 grain boats loaded with over 4 million *dan* of grain travelled to Beijing via Xuzhou every year. In the city lies Yongfu granary, Yongcheng depot and reserve granary. Outside are Changping granary, Xuzhou's Weitun granary and Guangyun granary, of which Guangyun granary is the largest one.

Dezhou Granary In 1129 AD, the Jin government built Jiangling granary in Dezhou, and later the Yuan government set up Lingzhou granary. In the thirteenth year of the reign of Yongle during the Ming dynasty, the Ministry of Revenue established Dezhou granary, which was responsible for collecting, storing and transporting grain from the provinces of Shandong and Henan. Jinan Prefecture established Guangji granary near Dezhou granary. Guangji granary collected grain and partially transported to the capital, what remained supplied for the troop.

Tianjin Military Grain City In the Ming dynasty, an enormous number of troops were stationing in Jizhou which served as a strategic military hub. Most of their provisions came from the Yangtze River and Huaihe River drainage area. When the canal froze in winter in the north, grain from the south had to be transported from north by sea to the military grain transit granaries near the Haihe River estuary. It was then transshipped to Beijing and other places. Tianjin was also called the Military Grain City because of its location at the north-south

徐州入京的漕船达12000多艘，漕粮400多万担。城内设有永福仓、永城库、预备仓等，城外有常平仓、徐州卫屯仓和广运仓，其中广运仓最大。

德州仓 公元1129年，金政权在德州建将陵仓。后来元政府在这里设立了陵州仓。明永乐十三年，中央户部建德州仓，负责征收、贮运山东、河南两省的漕粮。济南府在德州仓附近设立了广积仓，将当地收储的粮食，一部分运至京都，一部分留贮供军饷调出。

天津军粮城 明时，蓟州为军事要地，驻守重兵，军队的给养大部分来自江淮。南粮北调，北方冬季运河结冰时，必须借助海路北运至海河入海口附近的军粮转运仓，再转输到北京等地，地处南北水运枢纽的天津由此得名"军粮城"。

三、漕运路道与运行

中国的大江大河多是由西往东流，在陆路交通不发达的年代，开辟一条纵贯南北的运输水路，其重要意义是显而易见的。

隋朝开凿的通济渠，开南北交通之先河，为促进经济社会发展起到了重要作用。公元608年，隋炀帝大业四年，开凿永济渠，北通涿郡。公元610年，隋炀帝大业六年，开通江南河，自京口至余杭，形成了贯通南北的大运河。唐朝诗人皮日休在《汴河铭》中赞道："北通涿郡之渔商，南运江都之转输，其为利也博哉。"漕运的昌盛促进了南北的物流，成就了王朝帝都的繁华和辉煌，以致宋朝就有"天下转漕，仰此一渠"之说。元朝开通了京杭大运河，漕粮可直达大都，把漕运舟楫之便提升到新的高度，运输规模更大，水路更畅，使这一经济大动脉更加活跃，流通更为繁荣。

公元1282年，元世祖至元十九年，还初通了海路漕运。

历代漕运主要关涉国家的三个中心地区，即政治中心、军事中心和

water transport hub.

III. The Route and Operation of Water Transportation

Most of China's large rivers flow from west to east. In the age of underdeveloped land transport, the construction of a longitudinal north-south transport waterway was essential.

The Tongji Canal, built in the Sui dynasty, was the first to connect the northern and southern traffic, playing an important role in promoting economic and social development. In the 4th year of Emperor Yang's reign (608 AD), Yongji Canal was extended to Zhuojun in the north 2 years later, and the Jiangnan Canal was built to connect Jingkou and Yuhang, which formed a grand canal running through the north and the south. Pi Rixiu, a poet of Tang dynasty, praised the Grand Canal in his "Inscription on Bianhe River": "Expanding the fishing business to Zhuojun in the north, and transporting cargo from Jiangdu, the Grand Canal brings so many benefits!" The prosperity of caoyun promoted the logistics between the north and the south, and made the imperial capital flourish and magnificent. It was for this reason that the Song dynasty saying "both land way and water way transport of the country rely on this canal only" came into being. The Grand Canal of Beijing and Hangzhou was opened in the Yuan dynasty, which enabled grain to reach Dadu directly. The Grand Canal made the caoyun system even more encompassing. The scale of good transportation was greater and the waterway was smooth, which made this economic artery busier and prosperous.

In Zhiyuan 19 years (1282 AD) of Emperor Shizu in the Yuan dynasty, the transport by sea was initially opened.

In each dynasty, caoyun revolved around three areas of the country, which were the political center, the military center and the economic center. The large cities and major military towns were the main destinations for state grain, while the main grain producing and exporting areas represented the nation's economic centers. These three central regions changed with the different power shifts, as well as the changes of caoyun routes, ship management styles, grain varieties, transport seasons, and grain quantities. Such changes also painted some exquisitely colourful

经济中心。通都大邑和军事重镇是漕运官粮的主要目的地，而生产粮食、输出漕粮的主要地区则是国家的经济中心。这三个中心地区随着政权的更替屡次变迁，因而漕运线路、船舶管理和漕粮品种、运输季节、调运数量等都有不同，由此构成了一幅绚丽缤纷的漕运历史长卷。漕运保证了京师和北方军民所需粮食，促进了国家统一，同时，因运粮兼带商货，也推动了南北商品流通和经济交流。

当时，征收漕粮的主要地区有江、浙、赣、皖、湘、鄂、豫、鲁等省。漕粮的流向，也就是漕运的路径，主要是由东向西、由南至北、由东南到西北等。

明景泰二年（公元 1451 年），朝廷始设漕运总督，管理漕粮的取齐、上缴、监押运输，督促南方粮食经漕运至京师。清承明制，漕运体制仍沿袭未改，由漕台（漕运总督的别称）受理中国漕运事务。

总督漕运部院
Administrative Office of the Caoyun Governor

四、"南粮北调"与"北粮南运"

由于自然、历史、社会等方面诸多因素的叠加作用，历史上中国粮

miniatures on the canvas of China's grain history. The caoyun system ensured that the grain needed by the troops and the people in the capital and northern area was provided, while simultaneously driving the unification of the country. As a central means of goods transportation, caoyun also promoted economic exchanges between the north and the south.

At that time, the main areas for caoyun grain collection included the provinces of Jiangsu, Zhejiang, Jiangxi, Anhui, Hunan, Hubei, Henan and Shandong. The journey of grain reflected the flow of the rivers, from the east to the west, the south to the north, and the southeast to the northwest.

In the second year of Jingtai government in the Ming dynasty (1451 AD), the imperial government established the position of Caoyun Governor, who would be responsible for collecting grain and seeing that the government received it, transporting the grain, and overseeing the transport of southern grain to the capital. In the Qing dynasty, a similar grain transport system was adopted, and the Caotai (another name for the Caoyun Governor) handled China's grain transport affairs.

IV. The Grain Transfer of South-to-North and North-to-South

Throughout history, the nature of China's grain production has long been characterized by abundance in the south, the crop failure in the north, and the transfer of grain from the south to the north. The South enjoyed relative stability for a period of 500 years from the time of the Eastern Han dynasty onward. Thanks to such stability and the inheritance production techniques, the southern grain economy developed rapidly, and the grain grew abundantly. In the twenty-second year (724 AD) of the reign of Emperor Xuanzong in the Tang dynasty, the "Grain transport" started. In the second year of Emperor Guangde in the Tang dynasty (764 AD), Liu Yan played the role of transshipment envoy between Henan province and the Yangtze-Huaihe River drainage basin, and developed the transport of grain from the south to the north. Soon after, due to the destructive string of wars and famines in the north, production was suffered which led to a shortage of grain. For a long time, the southern grain was needed to alleviate northern famine crises. The reign of Emperor Shizu in the Yuan dynasty (1260—

食产销曾经长期呈现南丰北歉、南粮北调的传统格局。尤其是自东汉以后，南方地区有五百多年处于相对安定的环境，由于粮食生产的连续性和继承性，使得南方粮食经济迅猛发展，朝野粮足库盈，自用有余。公元724年，唐玄宗开元二十二年，始开"漕运南粮"。公元764年，唐代宗广德二年，刘晏为河南、江淮转运使，发展了南粮北运。之后，历代由于北方战祸连绵、灾荒不断，导致生产不振，产需失衡，粮食一直处于供不应求的状态之中，长期依靠南方的粮食来缓解危机，消除饥荒，至元世祖时期（公元1260年－1294年），南粮北运最多的年份，达350万石。这种局面经多次改朝换代也没有得到根本改观，维持了相当长的历史时期。

新中国成立后，直到改革开放前，国家粮食供给整体仍是南粮北调形势。改革开放后，实行农村生产责任制，农业生产力水平不断提高，生产供给增强，农业综合开发，商品粮基地建设，农田水利设施改善提高，北方地区，尤其是黑龙江等省区各种粮食作物特别是水稻种植面积扩大、产量高、品质好，消费覆盖面不断扩展，促使原来"南粮北调"的态势逆转为"北粮南运"。20世纪90年代以来，中国北方地区销往南方地区的粮食年平均超过2600万吨，占当年北方地区粮食总产量的12%。

1294 AD) saw the largest amounts of southern grain transported to the north with total haulage for that period at 3.5 million *dan*. This imbalance remained the status quo for a long period though the various dynasties changed.

After the establishment of the People's Republic of China, before the reform and opening up, the transportation of grain still followed the old pattern of south to north distribution. After the reform and opening up, the rural production responsibility was implemented, and the agricultural productivity improved. Production capacity and overall agricultural development improved in tandem with the establishment of a foundation for commodity grain. Irrigation works and water conservancy facilities moved forward in leaps and bounds. In north provinces, such as Heilongjiang, the planting area of various grain crops especially rice expanded, yields increased and quality improved. The size of the market for its consumption also grew significantly. The policy reversed the age-old south to north grain distribution paradigm. Since the 1990s, annually north to south grain sales have exceeded 26 million tons, accounting for 12% of the yearly total grain output of northern China.

第四章

中国粮策

Chapter 4

China's Grain Policy

粮食安全是世界和平与发展的重要保障，是构建人类命运共同体的重要基础，关系人类永续发展和前途命运。联合国粮农组织（UNFAO）发布2019年全球粮食展望报告，2019年世界谷物产量创新纪录，达27.22亿吨，较上一年增长2.7%，谷物利用量上涨1.5%，谷物消费量增长1.1%。但是，全球粮食损失与浪费惊人，报告发布粮食损失指数初步估计显示，全球约14%的粮食在从生产至零售环节之前被损失掉。报告指出，人们实际上对粮食损失和浪费的数量、位置和原因所知甚少，而可持续发展目标要求到2030年将全球零售和消费层面的人均食品浪费减半，并减少生产和供应链上的食品损失。因此，呼吁世界各国采取行动，减少粮食损失和浪费，政策制定者需要明确对减少浪费产生最有效的影响。中国，以不足世界10%的耕地，养活了占世界22%的人口，是全球粮食产量最大的国家，也是粮食进口最大的国家。

一、中国粮食安全特色之路

民为国基，谷为民命。粮食事关国运民生，粮食安全是国家安全的重要基础。新中国成立后，中国始终把解决人民吃饭问题作为治国安邦的首要任务。中国人口占世界的近1/5，粮食产量约占世界的1/4。中国依靠自身力量端牢自己的饭碗，实现了由"吃不饱"到"吃得饱"并且"吃得好"的历史性转变。这既是中国人民自己发展取得的伟大成就，也是为世界粮食安全做出的重大贡献。

主要粮食作物
Major Grain Crops

Grain security is an essential guarantee for world peace and development, a significant foundation for a global community of shared future, and an influential factor for the development and future of humanity. According to the Food Outlook issued by the UN's Food and Agriculture Organization (UNFAO), world grain production in 2019 hit a record of 2.722 billion tons, an increase of 2.7% on the previous year. Grain utilization will rise by 1.5 % and grain consumption by 1.1 %. Global food loss and waste are staggering. However, the preliminary estimates of the report's food loss index show that about 14% of the world's food is lost before it reaches retail. The report notes that little is actually known about the amount, location and cause of food loss and waste. Sustainable Development Goals call for halving food waste per capita globally during retail and consumption by 2030, and reducing food loss in production and along the supply chain. Calling on countries around the world to take action to reducing food loss and waste, policy makers need to identify the most effective means of waste reduction. China, which feeds 22 % of the world's population with less than 10 % of the world's arable land, is the world's largest grain producer and importer.

I. Grain Security in China

People are the foundation of a nation, and grain is our primary need. National prosperity and people's wellbeing depends on the presence of grain. Grain security is therefore a major prerequisite for national security. Since the founding of the People's Republic of China (PRC) in 1949, China has always prioritized grain security in state governance. With one fifth of the world's population, China accounts for a quarter of total global grain production. China is self-reliant in securing its own grain supply. Chinese people not only have sufficient grain to survive, but also enjoy a great amount of choice in what they eat. From being a nation riven by starvation, the Chinese people have transformed their nation through hard work and development. China's example to the world stands as a great contribution to global grain security.

Working according to its own national conditions, China has embarked on a road to establishing grain security by implementing innovative, coordinated, green, open, and inclusive development. This journey has stuck to high-quality

中国立足本国国情、粮情，贯彻创新、协调、绿色、开放、共享的新发展理念，落实高质量发展要求，实施新时期国家粮食安全战略，走出了一条中国特色粮食安全之路。

1. 稳步提升粮食生产能力

实施中国土地利用总体规划，从严管控各项建设占用耕地特别是优质耕地，健全建设用地"增存挂钩"机制，实行耕地占补平衡政策，严守 12000 万公顷耕地红线。全面落实永久基本农田特殊保护制度，划定永久基本农田 10300 多万公顷。目前，中国耕地面积 13488 万公顷，粮食作物播种面积达到 11700 多万公顷，夯实了粮食生产基础。

2. 保护和调动粮食种植积极性

保障种粮农民收益。粮食生产不仅是解决粮食需求问题，更是解决农民就业问题的重要途径和手段。中国农业人口规模巨大，通过城镇化减少农业人口将是一个渐进的过程，在这个过程中必须保障农民的就业和收入。为全面促进农村经济社会的发展，国家相继取消牧业税、生猪

粮食生产
Grain Production

development standards and to realize a national grain security strategy for a new era.

1. Steadily increasing grain production capacity

The Chinese government has implemented an overall plan for land use throughout the country. It strictly controls the occupation of cultivated land, especially high-quality land. It is improving the mechanism for ensuring that new construction land is approved when absolutely necessary, and implementing a policy of balancing the occupation and replenishment of arable land, thereby drawing a red line for the protection of its 120 million hectares of cultivated land. A complete, special protection system for permanent basic farmland has been implemented, and more than 103 million hectares of permanent basic farmland have been designated. There are more than 117 million hectares sown with grain, which represents an increase of about 4.5 million hectares since 1996. Therefore, the foundations of grain production have been strengthened.

2. Cultivating and enthusiasm for grain

The farming income should be guaranteed. Grain production not only makes an essential contribution to the task of feeding the people, but also provides employment to farmers. Since China has a huge agricultural population, the reduction of the arable population through urbanization will be a gradual process, during the course of which the employment and income of farmers must be guaranteed. In order to aid the all-round development of the rural economy and society, China has abolished the animal husbandry tax, pig slaughtering tax, tax on agricultural and forestry specialties and various other taxes. Significantly, in 2006, China abolished the agricultural tax, which had existed for 2,600 years. All these efforts have fundamentally reduced the burden on farmers. We will gradually adjust and improve the grain price formation mechanism as well as agricultural support and protection policies, and improve farmers' ability to resist natural and market risks through the implementation of land fertility protection subsidies for cultivated land and subsidies for the purchase of agricultural machinery and equipment. It is with such policies that we will guarantee the basic income of farmers, cultivate their enthusiasm for growing grain, and ensure the sustainable development of agriculture.

屠宰税和农林特产税，特别是在 2006 年全面取消了在中国存在 2600 年的农业税，从根本上减轻了农民的负担。逐步调整、完善粮食价格形成机制和农业支持保护政策，通过实施耕地地力保护补贴和农机具购置补贴等措施，提高农民抵御自然风险和市场风险的能力，保障种粮基本收益，保护农民种粮积极性，确保农业可持续发展。

3. 创新完善粮食市场体系

积极构建多元市场主体格局。深化国有粮食企业改革，鼓励发展混合所有制经济，促进国有粮食企业跨区域整合，打造骨干粮食企业集团。推动粮食产业转型升级，培育大型跨国粮食集团，支持中小粮食企业发展，促进形成公平竞争的市场环境。积极引导多元主体入市，市场化收购比重不断提高，粮食收购主体多元化格局逐步形成。

4. 健全完善国家宏观调控

注重规划引领。编制《中华人民共和国国民经济和社会发展第十三个五年规划纲要》《国家粮食安全中长期规划纲要（2008—2020 年）》《全国新增 1000 亿斤粮食生产能力规划（2009—2020 年）》《中国食物与营养发展纲要（2014—2020 年）》《全国农业可持续发展规划（2015—2030 年）》《全国国土规划纲要（2016—2030 年）》《国家乡村振兴战略规划（2018—2022 年）》《粮食行业"十三五"发展规划纲要》等一系列发展规划，从不同层面制定目标、明确措施，引领农业现代化、粮食产业以及食物营养的发展方向，多维度维护国家粮食安全。

5. 大力发展粮食产业经济

加快推动粮食产业转型升级。紧紧围绕"粮头食尾""农头工尾"，充分发挥加工企业的引擎带动作用，延伸粮食产业链，提升价值链，打造供应链，统筹建好示范市县、产业园区、骨干企业和优质粮食工程"四大载体"，在更高层次上提升国家粮食安全保障水平。

3. Innovating and improving the grain market system

A diverse market for grain should be built. China is further deepening its reform of state-owned grain enterprises, encouraging the development of a mixed ownership economy, promoting the cross-regional integration of state-owned grain enterprises, and creating backbone grain enterprise groups. China has been endeavored to transform and upgrade the grain industry, cultivate large transnational grain groups, support the development of small and medium-sized grain enterprises, and foster a market environment for fair competition. Besides, China has actively guided multiple players into the market, and the proportion of market-based procurement has been increasing. A network of diversified grain purchasers has gradually taken shape.

4. Improving macroeconomic regulation

State planning and guidance should be paid more attention. China has formulated a series of plans, involving "The Outline of the Thirteenth Five-year Plan for National Economic and Social Development of the People's Republic of China" "The Outline of the Medium- and Long-term Plan for National Grain Security (2008—2020)" "The National Plan for an Increase of Production Capacity for 50 Billion Kilogram of Grain (2009—2020)" "The Outline of China's Food and Nutrition Development (2014—2020)" "National Agriculture Sustainable Development Plan (2015—2030)" "The National Land Planning Outline (2016—2030)" "The National Rural Vitalization Strategic Plan (2018—2022)", and "The Outline of the 13th Five-year Development Plan for the Food Industry". It is through such plans that China defines its goals and measures at different levels, and guides the agricultural modernization, the food nutrition, and the food industry, with the goal of safeguarding national grain security.

5. Developing the grain industry economy

The transformation and upgrading of the grain industry should be accelerated. China upholds the principle carefully regulating grain planting in relation to the actual needs of the market in a policy called "Plant before plate" and another policy called "Agriculture leading industry" whereby primary and secondary industries are comprehensively integrated to realize the intensive processing of agricultural products. In this way, we can give full play to the role of processing enterprises for the engines of the agricultural industry to extend the grain industry

6. 全面建立粮食科技创新体系

强化粮食生产科技支撑。深入推进玉米、大豆、水稻、小麦国家良种重大科研联合攻关，大力培育、推广优良品种。超级稻、矮败小麦、杂交玉米等高效育种技术体系基本建立，成功培育出数万个高产优质作物新品种新组合，实现了 5－6 次大规模更新换代，优良品种大面积推广应用，基本实现主要粮食作物良种全覆盖。中国科学家袁隆平培育的超级杂交稻单产达到每公顷近 18.1 吨，刷新了世界纪录。加快优质专用稻米和强筋弱筋小麦以及高淀粉、高蛋白、高油玉米等绿色优质品种选育，推动粮食生产从高产向优质高产并重转变。

超级稻
Super Rice

7. 着力强化依法管理合规经营

完善粮食安全保障法律法规。加快推进粮食安全保障立法，颁布和修订实施《农业法》《土地管理法》《土壤污染防治法》《水土保持法》《农村土地承包法》《农业技术推广法》《农业机械化促进法》《种子法》《农产品质量安全法》《进出境动植物检疫法》《农民专业合作社法》《基本

chain, upgrade the value chain, and consolidate the supply chain. We have an overall strategy to promote national grain with a four-pillar system. The pillars are demonstration cities and counties, industrial parks, backbone enterprises, and the Quality Grain Project.

6. Establishing a comprehensive innovation system for grain science and technology

Scientific and technological support for grain production should be strengthened. China has promoted research into improved varieties of corn, soybeans, rice and wheat, and made concerted efforts to cultivate and popularize the best varieties. Highly efficient technology is in place for the cultivation of super rice, dwarf male-sterile wheat, and hybrid corn, and tens of thousands of new combinations of high-yield and high-quality crop varieties have been successfully cultivated after five or six phases of major upgrading. These have been popularized and applied over large areas, covering almost all major grain crops. The per unit yield of super hybrid rice cultivated by Chinese scientist Yuan Longping has reached nearly 18.1 tons per hectare, setting a new world best. China will speed up the breeding of high-quality special rice, strong gluten and weak gluten wheat, green and high-quality varieties such as high starch, high protein and high oil corn, so that our grain production will be high yield and high quality.

7. Strengthening management and operations in accordance with the law

Laws and regulations on grain security should be improved. To accelerate grain security legislation, China has promulgated and revised the following laws and regulations: the Agricultural Law, the Land Administration Law, the Soil Pollution Prevention and Control Law, the Law on Soil and Water Conservation, the Rural Land Contracting Law, the Law on the Popularization of Agricultural Technology, the Law on Promotion of Agricultural Mechanization, the Seed Law, the Law on Quality and Safety of Agricultural Products, the Law on the Entry and Exit Animal and Plant Quarantine, Law on Farmers' Specialized Cooperatives, the Regulations on the Protection of Basic Farmland, the Regulations on Land Reclamation, the Regulations on Pesticide Administration, the Regulations on Plant Quarantine, and the Regulations on the Administration of Grain Circulation.

农田保护条例》《土地复垦条例》《农药管理条例》《植物检疫条例》《粮食流通管理条例》等法律法规。

二、中国粮食对外开放与国际合作

中国积极践行自由贸易理念，认真履行加入世界贸易组织承诺，主动分享中国的粮食市场资源，推动世界粮食贸易发展。不断深化粮农领域国际合作，积极参与世界粮食安全治理，为促进世界粮食事业健康发展、维护世界粮食安全做出了重要贡献。

1. 对外开放日益扩大

涉粮外资企业加工转化粮食数量、产品销售收入不断增加，2018年分别占到中国的 14.5%、17%。外资企业进入中国粮食市场的广度、深度不断拓展，在食用植物油、粮食加工转化等领域的份额不断增长，并向粮食收购市场、批发零售和主食品供应等方面延伸，成为促进中国粮食产业发展的重要力量。

2. 国际合作全面加强

1996 年以来，中国与联合国粮农组织实施了 20 多个多边南南合作项目，向非洲、亚洲、南太平洋、加勒比海等地区的近 30 个国家和地区派遣近 1100 人次粮农技术专家和技术员，约占联合国粮农组织南南合作项目派出总人数的 60%。积极支持国内有条件的企业"走出去"，秉持共商共建共享原则，在有需要的国家和地区开展农业投资，推广粮食生产、加工、仓储、物流、贸易等技术和经验。截至 2017 年底，中国农业对外投资存量 173.3 亿美元，在境外设立企业 851 家，分布于六大洲的 100 个国家（地区），雇佣外方员工 13.4 万人，为东道国增加就业、发展经济、改善民生做出了积极贡献。

II. Opening Up and International Cooperation of China's Grain

China is an active promoter of free trade and works hard to fulfill commitments to the WTO. Moreover, China shares its grain market to facilitate the world grain trade. By expanding international cooperation in grain and agriculture as well as actively participating in global grain security governance, China has made an important contribution to the healthy development of the world grain industry and to grain security.

1. More opening-up to come

Foreign-funded enterprises in China are processing more grain by the day, and their revenue has been steadily increasing. In 2018, foreign enterprises processed 14.5 percent of all China's grain, and earned 17 percent of the total grain processing revenue. Foreign-funded enterprises are becoming more involved in China's grain market. They have growing shares in edible vegetable oil and grain processing, and play a pivotal part in activities ranging from procurement, wholesale and retail, to staple food supply. They have become a key force in the development of China's grain industry.

2. Stronger international cooperation than ever

Since 1996, the Chinese government and the United Nations Food and Agriculture Organization (UNFAO) have jointly implemented more than 20 multilateral South-South cooperation programs, and sent 1,100 agricultural experts and technical personnel to around 30 countries and regions in Africa, Asia, the South Pacific, and the Caribbean, accounting for 60 percent of the total number of personnel dispatched by the UNFAO's south-south cooperation program. Such programs support competent grain enterprises in their efforts to go global, encourage them to invest in agriculture in countries and regions where such investment is needed, and share technology and experience with them in the areas of grain production, processing, storage, logistics, and trade in accordance with the principles of extensive consultation, joint contribution and shared benefits. By the end of 2017, China had a total investment of 17.33 billion US dollars in agriculture overseas, with 851 enterprises operating in 100 countries and regions in 6 continents, employing 134,000 foreign employees. They have

三、中国粮食未来展望与政策主张

当前，中国粮食连年丰收、库存充裕、供应充足、市场稳定，粮食安全形势持续向好。展望未来，中国有条件、有能力、有信心依靠自身力量筑牢国家粮食安全防线。国家粮食安全保障政策体系基本成型，全面实施国家粮食安全战略，依靠自己保口粮，集中国内资源保重点，使粮食之基更牢靠、发展之基更深厚、社会之基更稳定。农业供给侧结构性改革尚有很大空间，粮食科技进步、单产提高、减少损失浪费、利用非粮食食物等方面还有较大潜力可供挖掘。充足的粮食储备可以保障粮食市场供应和市场基本稳定，现代化的粮食仓储物流体系可以防止出现区域性、阶段性粮食供给紧张问题，市场机制充分发挥作用能够解决品种结构矛盾。

1. 提高粮食生产能力

坚守耕地保护红线，节约和高效利用水资源。不断提高耕地质量，到 2022 年，确保建成 6667 万公顷高标准农田。到 2035 年，粮食种植面积保持总体稳定。加快推进节水供水重大水利工程建设，不断完善农田水利设施，提高水资源利用效率。

2. 加强储备应急管理

加强粮食储备管理。以服务宏观调控、调节稳定市场、应对突发事件和提升国家安全能力为目标，科学确定粮食储备功能和规模，改革完善粮食储备管理体制，健全粮食储备运行机制，强化内控管理和外部监督，加快构建更高层次、更高质量、更有效率、更可持续的粮食安全保障体系。

helped these countries and regions to create more jobs, develop their economy, and improve peoples' lives.

III. Prospects and Policies of China's Grain

China has recently enjoyed a run of good harvests, sufficient grain supplies and reserves, and a stable grain market. Such a situation is indicative of increased grain security. Looking to the future, China has the conditions, capabilities and confidence determination to enhance grain security. A national system of grain security guarantee policies is in place. China's grain strategy in the new era consists of ensuring security of grain through food self-sufficiency, pooling domestic resources to ensure key links in grain security, and securing the grain supply as a foundation for national development and social stability. There is plenty of space for supply-side structural reform in China's agriculture industry and plenty of room for progress in China's agro-technology, in terms of increasing per unit area yield, reducing food waste, and developing non-grain foods. Adequate grain reserves help ensure market supply and guarantee market stability. A modernized grain storage and logistics system helps prevent regional or provisional grain supply crises. Market mechanisms in full play help improve the structure of grain varieties.

1. Enhancing grain productivity

We should keep to the red line for the protection of cultivated land, save and utilize water resources efficiently. By 2022, China will complete the construction of 66.67 million ha of high-standard farmland, and by 2035, it's ratio for land dedicated to grain planting will remain stable. China will implement major hydro construction projects for water conservation and supply, improve farmland hydro facilities, and increase water resource utilization efficiency.

粮食收获
Grain Harvest

3. 建设现代粮食流通体系

加快建设现代粮食流通体系。坚持市场化改革取向与保护农民利益并重，以确保口粮绝对安全、防止"谷贱伤农"为底线，适应世界贸易组织规则，积极稳妥地推进粮食收储制度和价格形成机制改革，充分发挥市场配置粮食资源的决定性作用，更好地发挥政府作用，使粮价更好地反映市场供求，激发市场活力，促进供需平衡，加快形成统一开放、竞争有序的现代粮食流通体系。

4. 积极维护世界粮食安全

继续深入推进南南合作，为实现联合国 2030 年可持续发展目标中的"消除饥饿，实现粮食安全，改善营养状况和促进可持续农业"做出积极努力。

深化与共建"一带一路"国家的粮食经贸合作关系，共同打造国际粮食合作新平台，促进沿线国家的农业资源要素有序自由流动、市场深度融合。

凡益之道，与时偕行。进入新时代，中国人民更加关注食物的营养

2. Improving the management of emergency grain reserves

The management of grain reserves should be improved. To facilitate macro-regulation, a steady market, sound emergency response, and national security, China will apply scientific rationale when designing the functions and scale of grain reserves. It will reform and complete its management mechanisms, improve its operating mechanisms, and strengthen internal management and external supervision. The goal is to build a grain security guarantee system, which is more advanced, effective, efficient and sustainable.

3. Building a modern grain circulation system

A modern grain circulation system should be built with stepping up efforts. China places equal importance on market-oriented reform and the protection of farmers' interests. Upholding its red line of absolute security for staple food and zero risks for farmers of low grain prices, China will adapt itself to WTO rules, actively and steadily reform its grain purchase and storage systems as well as pricing mechanisms, giving full play to the decisive role of the market in allocating grain resources, and letting the government play its role better. Through these measures, China hopes that grain prices can better reflect market demand and supply, that market vitality will be boosted, and a balance between demand and supply can be achieved to form a unified and open, modern grain circulation system in which competition is fair.

4. Safeguarding global grain security

South-South cooperation should be advanced. China will work hard to achieve the United Nations 2030 Agenda for Sustainable Development goals to "end hunger, achieve grain security, improve nutrition and promote sustainable agriculture".

Enhancing grain trade cooperation with the countries along the routes of the Belt and Road, together, we will establish a new international platform for grain cooperation to facilitate the free and orderly flow of agricultural resources and deepen the integration of markets in the Belt and Road countries.

An ancient Chinese wisdom has it that all good principles should adapt to changing times if they are to remain relevant. In the new era, the Chinese people are more concerned with their nutrition and health. Before, people worried about having enough to eat, but now, they worry about the quality and safety of the

与健康,既要"吃得饱",更要"吃得好""吃得放心"。初心不忘,人民至上。中国将在习近平新时代中国特色社会主义思想指引下,始终以人民对美好生活的向往为奋斗目标,牢固树立总体国家安全观,深入实施国家粮食安全战略和乡村振兴战略,进一步加强粮食生产能力、储备能力、流通能力建设,推动粮食产业高质量发展,提高国家粮食安全保障能力,为人民获得更多福祉奠定坚实根基。

确保粮食安全,中国与世界命运休戚与共。中国将继续遵循开放包容、平等互利、合作共赢的原则,努力构建粮食对外开放新格局,与世界各国一道,加强合作,共同发展,为维护世界粮食安全做出不懈努力,为推动构建人类命运共同体做出新的贡献。

粮食安全
Grain Security

5. 未来粮食科技发展展望

未来十年,国际上将围绕系统认知分析、精准动态感知、数据科学、基因编辑、微生物组五大关键技术寻求农业领域的科技突破。这同样是未来中国农业领域必须努力、不可或缺的关键核心技术。同时,立

food. The people's needs are the highest responsibility of the Chinese government. In line with Xi Jinping Thought on Socialism with Chinese Characteristics for a New Era, China will see that the people are able to realize their expectations for a better life. Pursuing a holistic approach to national security, China will further implement its national strategies for grain security and rural vitalization. In order to provide greater well-being for the people, China will increase grain productivity, boost grain reserves, and improve grain circulation, to facilitate the high-quality development of its grain industries and strengthen the guarantees of grain security.

China is part of the global effort to ensure grain security. Under the principle of openness, inclusiveness, equality, mutual benefit, and win-win cooperation, China will embrace a new situation of opening up with regard to grain issues. In pursuit of common development, China continues to enhance cooperation with other nations to safeguard global grain security, as a contribution to building a global community of shared future.

5. Outlook on future development of grain technology

In next decade, the world will seek to make scientific and technological breakthroughs in the agricultural field, which centers on the five key technologies of systematic cognitive analysis, precise dynamic perception, data science, gene editing and microbiomes. China's agricultural sector must similarly strive to in its research into these core technologies in the future. In consideration of China's barren and inferior land resources, Chinese scientists still need to make breakthroughs in several important fields that will transform the present, lead the future and shape our era-breakthroughs of importance to the scientific community such as the life of mountains, rivers, forests, farmland, lakes and grass, land resource security and modern engineering, and technical control. Focusing on the scientific and technological system of precise investigation, careful monitoring and smart management, breakthroughs will be made in key core technologies, such as big data for cultivated land quality, cultivated land health diagnosis technology, ecological fertile farmland construction technology, soil biodiversity protection and cultivated land conservation technology, and cultivated land system evolution simulation technology. Restoration and improvement will be carried out in key areas, such as the overall protection of black soil, the restoration of the Yellow

足中国地薄质劣的资源国情，中国科学家还需要在几个颠覆现在、引领未来、开创时代的重要领域，在山水林田湖草生命共同体重大科学问题、土地资源安全与管控现代工程技术难题上取得突破。聚焦精准调查、精细感知、精明治理的科学技术体系，在一些关键核心技术上取得突破进展，比如耕地质量大数据、耕地健康诊断技术、生态良田构建技术、土壤生物多样性保护和耕地养护技术、耕地系统演化模拟仿真技术；对一些重点区域进行修复治理，比如黑土地整体保护、黄河流域系统修复、盐碱地沙土地综合治理；在国家发展的重大需求方面全力以赴，比如全球变化与低碳耕作制度研究、耕地资源智慧监测等。新一轮科技革命和产业正在重构全球创新版图，需要规划好未来技术发展的路线图，明确创新主攻方向，确定耕地资源是不可或缺的一环。

四、现代粮食科技创新——中国粮谷

建设中国粮谷，是贯彻习近平总书记"延伸粮食产业链、提升价值链、打造供应链""扛稳粮食安全的重任"指示和中央区域经济布局对河南要求的具体行动。中国粮谷，是以粮食产后科技创新为目标，汇聚粮食产业资源，实现人才、科技、资本有机统一，组建的粮食科技集成示范区。通过科技创新提升对粮食产业经济的支撑能力，加速河南粮食强省动力转换，为"粮食安全""供给侧结构性改革""乡村振兴"等国家战略实施和融入"一带一路"建设贡献智慧。

粮食安全是国家战略。粮食乃安天下之本。粮食安全，既是口粮、谷物、食物的安全，又是产能、供应、品质的安全；其内涵涉及育种、种植、收获、储运、加工、包装、供应等多个环节，涵盖农、工、商诸多领域。粮食是一个"农头工身食尾"的产业链条，与发达国家相比，我国粮食产业呈现出"头昂身凹尾不起"的结构性非平齐格局。对粮食产业进行精准的供给侧结构性改革，关键是要以科技为引领，突出

River drainage area system, and the comprehensive treatment of saline-alkali and sandy soil. There will be a focus on major national development requirements, such as global change and low-carbon farming systems, and the smart monitoring of arable land resources. A new round of scientific and technological revolution in industry is reconstructing the global innovation landscape. It is necessary to plan the road map for future technological development, clarify the main direction for innovation, and determine the farmland resources as an indispensable part.

IV. Modern Grain Scientific Technology Innovation— China's Grain Valley

The construction of China's Grain Valley represents an implementation of General Secretary Xi Jinping's instructions to "Extend the grain industry chain, upgrade the value chain, build the supply chain" and "Carry out the heavy task of stabilizing grain security". As an integrated demonstration zone of grain science and technology, China's Grain Valley is well suited to the requirements of the central regional economic layout for Henan, which focuses on grain post-harvest technological innovation, concentrating the resources of grain industry and realizing the organic unification of talent, science and technology, and capital. Through scientific and technological innovation, we will enhance the backbone role of the grain economy, boost the momentum behind Henan's transformation into a powerful grain province, and contribute wisdom to the implementation of national strategies such as the strategies for "grain security" "supply-side structural reform" "rural revitalization" and the construction of "The Belt and Road".

Grain security is a national strategy. As we know that food is the foundation of peace. While grain security is not only the security of grain, cereal and food, but also the security of productivity, supply, and quality, which involves breeding, planting, harvesting, storage and transportation, processing, packaging and supply. Therefore, it underpins agriculture, industry and business. China's grain industry represents a chain with agriculture at the start, industry in the middle, and food at the end. Compared with developed countries, China's grain industry presents itself unevenly with an abundance of grain, an underdeveloped processing industry, and a food output, which is much lower than it should be. The key to carrying

创新发展、转型升级、提质增效，以带动大粮农产业进步。在发展动能上，要激发粮食产业技术创新活力，增强技术装备升级的驱动力，促进新产品、新模式、新业态的加速成长；在发展路径上，以信息化区块链技术在产业场景的应用为引领，发挥粮食产业供应链的引擎作用，协同联动，融合发展，形成"大粮食""大产业""大市场""大流通"格局；在发展目标上，以品质安全、健康营养、效益提高为抓手，进一步增加绿色优质序列化粮食产品供给，促进粮食产业链延伸、价值链提升及供应链再造，加快推动产业迈向中高端水平，在更高层次上保障国家粮食安全。

中国粮谷建设，以园区管理体制机制创新为基础，通过要素集聚、链条配套、服务优化、文化传播等功能叠加，优化科技创新生态，聚焦生物技术、信息技术、装备智能化、绿色加工、产业标准化五个重点，在粮食产后收储、加工、包装、物流、供应等环节的关键技术上寻求突破；打通基础研究与应用研发、应用研发与商业推广、商业推广与风投资本的衔接通道，实现科学研究基础设施、技术研发共性平台、国际合作渠道的共享；在基于生物技术的产品链变革、基于信息技术的供应链再造、基于装备技术的产业升级、基于节能技术的减损保质、基于标准化技术的产业升级五个方面发挥推动作用。中国粮谷建设始终坚持习近平总书记提出的四个"需要"，加快科技创新，推动粮食产业高质量发展，构建发展新格局，为提高人民的生活品质和顺利开启全面建设社会主义现代化国家新征程提供坚实基础。

中国粮谷建设，以国家和省部重大研发需求、开放实验室建设、粮食经济战略研究、粮食基础理论研究、粮食文化传承发展为载体，在科研中试、技术服务、科技转化、企业总部等方面提供保障，强化创业、孵化、培训、知识产权交易功能，实现科技与资本高度融合，实现粮食核心关键技术、重大共性技术、卡脖子技术的实质性突破，为粮食科学

out targeted supply-side structural reform in our grain industry is to take science and technology as the guide, highlight innovative development, transformation and upgrading, and improve the quality and efficiency of the grain industry, so as to promote the progress of the big food and agriculture industry. In terms of development momentum, it is necessary to stimulate technological innovation in the grain industry, strengthen the driving force for the upgrade of technological equipment, and accelerate the growth of new products, new models and new forms of business. In terms of development path, the application of information block chain technology in industry should take the lead. We should give play to the engine-like role of the grain industry supply chain, and ensure that the well-coordinated development provides a scale up in terms of grain products, the size of the industry and the market including the variety of channels of circulation. In terms of development goals, we will further increase the supply of green and high-quality serialized grain products, promote the extension of the grain industry chain, continue to make improvements to the value chain as we reconstruct the supply chain, accelerate the movement toward middle and high-end level industry, and ensure to make breakthroughs in national grain security.

The way in which China's Grain Valley development will be managed will optimize the ecology of scientific and technological innovation through the superposition of functions such as factor agglomeration, chain supporting, service optimization and cultural dissemination, focusing on the five key points of biotechnology, information technology, intelligent equipment, green processing and industrial standardization. We will make breakthroughs in the key technologies of post-harvest grain storage, processing, packaging, logistics and supply. In addition, we will connect basic research with applied research and development, applied research and development with commercial promotion, and commercial promotion with venture capital, and realize a shared scientific research infrastructure, a common platform of technology research development and international cooperation channels. The Grain Valley will plays a driving role in five areas: product chain transformation based on biotechnology, supply chain reengineering based on information technology, industrial upgrading based on equipment technology, loss reduction and quality preservation based on energy-saving technology, and industrial upgrading based on standardized technology.

和产业技术持续发展提供源头动力。

中国粮谷建设采取"政府主导+科技引领+消费带动+产业驱动+市场运作"的运行模式，坚持"政产学研用金"融合，以市场需求为导向，以粮食科技创新为支撑，以粮食产业升级为抓手，以粮食产业经济高质量发展为目标；促进粮食供给侧结构性改革，促进农业、粮食、食品三体聚合，实现粮食产业链、价值链和供应链协同，在河南打造全球粮食科技的制高点、全国粮食产业创新的试验田、引领粮食经济高质量发展的航母群，为构建国家粮食安全保障体系夯实科学研究、技术进步、产业发展的基础。

习近平总书记提出的"四个面向"要求——"坚持面向世界科技前沿、面向经济主战场、面向国家重大需求、面向人民生命健康"，为中国粮谷发展过程中的科技创新指明了方向。中国粮谷模式下的粮食产业创新始终坚持需求导向和问题导向，加快推进能够快速突破、及时解决问题的技术，提前部署战略性的技术攻关；通过整合优化科技资源配置，对现有国家重点实验室进行重组，形成我国实验室体系，推进创新体系建设，进行优化组合，克服发展中分散、低效、重复的弊端。"民为邦本，本固邦宁。"人民是历史的创造者，是决定党和国家前途命运的根本力量。面向人民生命健康为粮食产业的发展提出了新的要求，中国粮谷以标准化建设为抓手，结合信息技术建立从农田到餐桌的全流程安全品质快检和数据分析系统，实现全部产品的可追溯，从"口"的角度保障人民生命健康。

China's Grain Valley has always adhered to the four "needs" put forward by General Secretary Xi Jinping, which has accelerated scientific and technological innovation, promoted the high-quality development of the grain industry. It also has established a new development model, providing a solid foundation for improving the quality of life of the people while smoothly facilitating our new journey of building a modern socialist country.

With national and provincial major research and development goals, open laboratory construction, strategic economic research, the basic theory research of grain, and grain culture heritage under its wings, the construction of China's Grain Valley strengthens entrepreneurship, incubation and training of talent, as well as intellectual property rights trading. It has facilitated a synergy between technology and capital, made substantive breakthroughs in grain core and key technologies, major generic technologies, and bottleneck technologies, so as to provide a source of impetus for the sustained development of grain science and industrial technologies.

The construction of China's Grain Valley will follow the formula of "the government guiding + technology leading + consumption stimulating + industry driving + market operating". Adhering to the methodology of IARAC (Government-Industry-Academia-Research-Application-Capital), the China's Grain Valley will be guided by market demand, supported by grain science and technology innovation, boosted by grain industry upgrading, and see high-quality and economic grain industry development as its goal. We will promote the supply-side structural reform of grain, promote the integration of agriculture, grain and food, realize the coordination of the grain industry chain, value chain and supply chain, build Henan province into a leader of global grain science and technology, a paradigm of national grain industry innovation, and a flagship leading the high-quality development of grain economy so as to build a national grain security system to consolidate the foundation of scientific research, technological progress, and industrial development.

General Secretary Xi Jinping has promulgated the concept of the "four fronts". That is the need for us to "face the frontier of science and technology, face the main economic battlefield, face the major needs of the country, and face the people's lives and health". Xi's words point out the direction of travel for scientific

改善科技创新生态,激发创新创造活力的根本在体制机制创新。要实现科研体制机制创新,首先要改变从事基础研究的广大高校、科研院体制机制创新,充分释放科研机构活力,我国才能实现真正的技术突破和飞跃。中国粮谷下辖研究院引入风投资本,实现基础研究、应用研发、商业推广的良性循环模式,建立新的利益分配链条,充分调动科研人员和技术发明者的创新动力。在经济从高速发展转向高质量发展中,打通粮食产业中支撑科技强国的创新链条。

and technological innovation in China's grain development. China's grain industry innovation under the China's Grain Valley model has always been demand-oriented and problem-oriented, accelerating the promotion of technology that can quickly break through and solve problems in time, while making strategic technological breakthroughs at the earliest opportunity. By integrating and optimizing the allocation of scientific and technological resources, existing state key laboratories should be reorganized to form China's laboratory system, promote the construction of innovation systems, optimize coordination, and overcome the disadvantages of decentralization, low efficiency and repetition in development. "The people are the foundation of a country, and the steadiness of the country relies on the stability of the people." The people are the creators of history and the fundamental force that determine the future and destiny of the Party and the country. Our new tasks should serve the development of grain industry that revolves around the axis of the people's lives and their health. China's Grain Valley takes standardized construction as the starting point and combines information technology to establish a system for rapid safety and quality inspection, and a data analysis system, which analyses the whole process from farmland to table to achieve traceability of all products and protect people's lives and health.

Institutional innovation is the key to improving the ecosystem for scientific and technological innovation and stimulating innovation and creativity. In order to realize the innovation of our scientific research system, we must first change institutional innovation in universities and colleges and in the scientific research institutes engaged in basic research, to fully release the vitality of scientific research institutions, so that China can realize real technological breakthroughs and leap forward. Research institutes affiliated with China's Grain Valley will introduce venture capital to realize a virtuous cycle model of basic research, applied research and development, and commercial promotion, to establish a new benefit distribution chain, and fully mobilize the innovative power of scientific researchers and technical inventors. In the transition from high-speed economic development to high-quality development, we should open up the innovation chain in the grain industry to support the development of science and technology.

第五章

中原粮谷

Chapter 5

Achievements of the Central Plains' Grain

民天至上，豫人钟情。生生不息的中华文明养育了中原大地热爱生活、勤劳朴实的芸芸众生。人们倾心粮作，励志图强，从古至今，续写了一幕幕彪炳史册的粮食辉煌。

中华人民共和国成立后，河南一直是中国粮食领域的重要支柱，实力雄厚，底气十足，长期受到党和国家莫大的政策支持，在粮食产能、粮食科技、粮食管理、粮食交易、粮食教育、粮食文化等方面都具有中国的领先水平。建国初期，国家就在河南建设了粮食专业的最高学府、国家部属的粮食科研所和粮食机械制造企业。改革开放后，国家在河南建设了中国第一个粮食交易批发市场、中国第一个粮食期货商品交易所、中国第一个粮食信息网等重要粮食机构。中国特色社会主义进入新时代以来，为了贯彻落实国家"建设社会主义文化强国"的战略和习近平"提高国家文化软实力，讲好中国故事"的指示精神，坚定文化自信，推动文化事业全面繁荣，河南省政府与国家粮食和物资储备局把中国粮食博物馆作为共建河南工业大学的重点项目，定位是国家级的行业博物馆、国家粮食文化中心。为落实习近平"延伸粮食产业链、提升价值链、打造供应链""扛稳粮食安全重任"的指示和中央区域经济布局的要求，河南正在筹建国家级粮食产学研基地——中国粮谷，通过科技创新提升对粮食产业经济的支撑能力，加速河南粮食强省动力转换，为"粮食安全""乡村振兴"和"一带一路"的国家战略实施贡献智慧。

Henan is China's kitchen. The timeless Chinese civilization has nurtured life-loving, hard-working and down-to-earth people of the Central Plain. They have always devoted themselves to grain harvesting endlessly. From ancient times to the present, they are the writers of the magnificent epic that is the history of Chinese grain.

Since the founding of the People's Republic of China, Henan has played an essential role in the development of China's grain industry. Thanks to a long history supporting policies from the Party and the state, Henan has grown stronger. Henan province leads in production capacity, science and technology, management, trade, education, culture, and in other areas of the grain industry. In the early days of the founding of the People's Republic of China, the state set up the supreme institute for grain studies, the Grain Research Institute, and the grain machinery manufacturing enterprise under the state ministry in Henan. After reform and opening up, the state built the first grain trading wholesale market, the grain futures commodity exchange, the grain information network and other important grain institutions in Henan, China. Since the implementation of socialism with Chinese characteristics into a new era, Henan Provincial Government and National Food and Strategic Reserves Administration have worked together on the construction of the China Grain Museum. The museum, a key addition to Henan University of Technology, operates as a national industry museum and grain culture center. The goal is to implement the state strategy of "setting up a socialist cultural power". The museum accords with Xi Jinping's plan to "improve national cultural soft power and share the real China with the world", to strengthen cultural self-confidence, and promote the prosperity of cultural undertakings. In order to realize Xi Jinping's vision for "extending the grain industry chain, upgrading the value chain and setting up the supply chain" and "shouldering the important task of stabilizing food security" and the Party Central Committee's requirements for the regional economic planning, Henan is preparing to set up a national grain industry. Its education and research base will be China Grain Valley. The Valley will improve its support capacity for the grain industry economy through scientific and technological innovation. A central task is to accelerate Henan's transformation into a strong grain-secure and prosperous province, which can share its wisdom as a national strategic contribution to the

一、最高粮食学府——郑州粮食学院

1956年6月，中华人民共和国粮食部在北京成立中央粮食干部学校，1959年初组建北京粮食专科学校，同年9月7日成立郑州粮食学院筹建处，并开始在郑州征购土地及建校工程。

1960年6月16日，粮食部在北京宣告中国第一所综合性的高等粮食学校郑州粮食学院正式成立，学校受粮食部和河南省双重领导，以粮食部为主。1960年8月15日，中华人民共和国国务院任命张靖为郑州粮食学院副院长，当月，北京粮食专科学校分3批搬迁至郑州。1960年9月1日，学校首次参加中国统一高考录取的320名新生报到，学校举行成立暨开学典礼，从此开启了中国粮食专业的高等教育。

任命书
Letter of Appointment

学校经过40多年的发展，于2004年5月13日组建成河南工业大学。河南工业大学是河南省人民政府和国家粮食局共建高校，先后隶属国家粮食部、商业部和国内贸易部；1959年开展本科教育，1981年开始硕士研究生教育，2013年开始博士研究生教育。学校坚持"扎根中原，立足行业，服务中国，面向世界"的办学定位，严守"育人为本、质量立校、特色发展"的办学理念，秉承"明德、求是、拓新、笃行"的校训，大力弘

development of the "Belt and Road Initiative".

I. Zhengzhou Grain College – the Supreme Grain Institution of China

The Central Grain Cadre School was established by the Ministry of Grain of the People's Republic of China in June 1956, and Beijing Grain College was established at the beginning of the year 1959 in Beijing. On September 7 of the same year, the Preparatory Office of Zhengzhou Grain College was established. It purchased land for the construction of the college in Zhengzhou.

On June 16, 1960, the Ministry of Grain in Beijing formally announced the establishment of Zhengzhou Grain College, which was the first comprehensive Grain College in China. The college was under the dual leadership of Ministry of Grain and Henan province, with the Ministry of Grain as the main body. On August 15, 1960, State Council of the People's Republic of China appointed Zhang Jing as vice president. In the same month, Beijing Grain College moved to Zhengzhou. On September 1, 1960, 320 students who had participated in the first China national College Entrance Examination were enrolled in the college. The college's inauguration ceremony symbolized the beginning of specialized grain related higher education in China.

After more than 40 years of development, the college was merged with Henan University of Technology on May 13, 2004. The university, jointly built by the Henan Provincial People's Government and National Food and the Strategic Reserves Administration, is a subordinate to Ministry of Grain, Ministry of Commerce and Ministry of Internal Trade successively. The university began undergraduate education in 1959, postgraduate education in 1981, and doctoral education in 2013. It adheres to the university's ethos that is to "take root in the central plains, base itself on the industry, serve China, and face the world", as well as prides itself on the cultivation of talent. Driven by its motto of "Virtue, Truth, Innovation, Experience", the university vigorously carries forward the principles of "Respecting science, Exploring persistently, Serving nation and education, and Pursuing self-improvement". Its spirit can be characterized by its aspiration for "unity and progress", coupled with "pragmatism and efficiency". Its teaching style

扬"崇尚科学、勇于探索、报国兴学、自强不息"的工大精神,凝练形成了"团结进取、务实高效"的校风、"博学奉献"的教风和"勤奋诚信"的学风。教师中,有国际标准化组织食品技术委员会谷物与豆类分会主席卞科教授、国际谷物科技协会主席王凤成教授、三届奥运会田径裁判王晏教授等知名专家,还有一批专家教授担任中国粮油学会、中国粮食工程建设委员会、中国高校博物馆专业委员会、中国磨料磨具标准化技术委员会、中国热处理学会、中国化学会有机化学磷化学专业委员会等学术组织理事长或副理事长职务,他们在各自专业领域和教学岗位上教书育人,竭诚奉献,堪称楷模。学校现有全日制在校生35000余人,其中研究生1600余人,外国留学生200余人。先后为社会输送了21万余名合格毕业生,粮食行业半数以上的管理精英和技术骨干均出自本校,被誉为粮食行业的"黄埔军校"。

二、首个粮食史馆——中国粮食博物馆

中国粮食博物馆是国家粮食局和河南省人民政府共建河南工业大学的重点项目,定位是国家级的行业博物馆。

中国粮食博物馆
China Grain Museum

is determined by the pursuit of erudition, and dedication, and it hopes to instill a culture of erudition and dedication in its students. The university counts a number of renowned experts among its teaching staff. There are Professor Bian Ke, chairman of the Cereal and Legume Branch of the International Organization for Standardization Food Technology Committee, Professor Wang Fengcheng, chairman of the International Association of Cereal Science and Technology, Professor Wang Yan, a three-time Olympic athletics judge of Track and Field. There are also a number of experts and professors serving as directors or vice-chairmen of academic organizations, such as the China Grain and Oil Society, the China Grain Engineering Construction Committee, the China University Museum Professional Committee, the China Abrasive and Abrasive Tool Standardization Technical Committee, the China Heat Treatment Society, and the Professional Committee of Phosphorus Chemistry of Organic Chemistry of Chinese Chemical Society. They are dedicated teachers and exemplary in their respective professional fields and the field of education. There are more than 35,000 full-time students including more than 1,600 graduate students and more than 200 foreign students. Over 210,000 qualified graduates have entered the industry. More than half of the management elites and the people who made up the technical backbone of the grain industry come from the university. It is known as the Huangpu Academy of the grain industry.

II. China Grain Museum—the First Grain History Museum

China Grain Museum is a key project of Henan University of Technology jointly built by National Food and Strategic Reserves Administration and Henan Provincial People's Government, with the aim of being a national industry museum.

粮食文化，博大精深。几年来，根据中华人民共和国国务院《博物馆条例》，围绕藏、研、展三大职能开展筹建工作，收集各种粮食文化资料 40 余万件，有力地保护了粮食文化遗产。《中国粮食博物馆展陈大纲》规划有十大基本陈展区，包括天地精华、谷脉流长、廪实仓盈、功济大千、流脂香韵、舌尖风光、枝蔓同根、文明之舟、粟海探幽、五洲粮缘等。

中国粮食博物馆设有三厅两区。天地精华展区重点展示了人类从狩猎时代和采摘时代到农业时代的过渡情况、五谷的概念、中国粮食作物的分布格局与演变、美洲粮食作物的引进和未来粮食发展等。电影厅专题片《粮食》讲述了粮食产生发展以及粮食和人类社会发展的关系、粮食的现状等等，提醒人们节粮爱粮、感恩粮食、敬畏粮食，这部电影是 2015 年国家粮食局举办的粮食科技周的主题片。文明之舟展区展示的是粮食与人类及人类社会发展的关系，主要有粮食与农业、粮食与战争、粮食与灾荒、粮食与粮证、粮食与民俗、粮食与文艺等方面的关系

中国粮食博物馆
China Grain Museum

中国粮食博物馆
China Grain Museum

China's grain culture is extensive and profound. Over the past few years, in accordance with the "Museum Regulations" of State Council of the People's Republic of China, preparatory work has been carried out in relation to the three major functions of collection, research and exhibition. The collection of more than 400, 000 represents a successful effort to protect the cultural heritage of grain in China. The "Exhibition Outline of China Grain Museum" plans to set up ten basic exhibition areas, including the Essence of Heaven and Earth, the Long River of the Grain Vein, Surplus of Millet and Rice, Great Achievements, the Fragrance of Abundance, the Imagery of Taste, the Root of the Branches and Vines, the Boat of Civilization, the Millet Sea, and the Grain Fate of the Five Continents.

There are three halls and two sections in the China Grain Museum. The Essence of Heaven and Earth exhibition area focuses on the transition of Chinese civilization from the hunter-gatherer phase into the agricultural era. The exhibition also describes the nature of the five kinds of grains (rice, wheat, soybean, corn, and potato), the evolution of China's grain crops, the introduction of American grain crops and the direction of grain development for the future. In the film hall, the feature film *Grain* explores the production and development of grain, the relationship between grain and the development of human society, the current state of the grain industry. The film reminds people to save, love, respect, and be grateful for grain, which was the highlight of Grain Science and Technology

和国家粮食管理机构沿革等。一部粮食史就是一部人类发展史。目前中国粮食博物馆已成为河南工业大学的特色文化中心,成为中国粮食文化交流的重要平台,已迎接游客数十万人次,迎来各地参观考察团体数百个,有力推动了中国粮食文化事业的发展。

2018年,中国粮食博物馆馆长师高民成为中国高校博物馆专业委员会副主任委员,同时授牌北京大学、北京航空航天大学、吉林大学、武汉大学、西北农林科技大学、广州中医药大学、中国传媒大学、河南工业大学、陕西师范大学、上海交通大学、清华大学、上海大学等12所大学为中国高校博物馆专业委员会主任、副主任委员单位。

三、首部粮食史书——《中国粮食史图说》

2016年春,由河南工业大学组织编撰的"十二五"国家重点图书出版规划项目《中国粮食史图说》出版发行,填补了中国史学空白,成为2016—2018年中国新华书店畅销书,受到粮食行业的一致好评,并成为中国粮食文化科普教育和粮食文化项目建设的重要参考文献。

《中国粮食史图说》
Chinese Grain History with Illustrations

国以民为本,民以食为天。粮食是人类赖以生产生活的基本要素,也是社会发展进步的首要物质资源。她汲取了天地的精华,和水一样成

Week held by the National Food and Strategic Reserves Administration in 2015. The Boat of Civilization exhibition examines the relationship between grain and people, between grain and the development of human society, and the ways in which grain has influenced human culture, in terms of agriculture, war, famine, grain certificates, folk customs, literature and art. The exhibition also considers the evolution of the national grain management organization. As it is said that the history of grain is the history of human development. The China Grain Museum is becoming the characteristic cultural center of Henan University of Technology, and an important platform for exchange on the subject of China's grain culture. The museum has welcomed hundreds of thousands of tourists as well as hundreds of visiting and inspection groups from all over the country to successfully promote the development of China's grain culture.

In 2018, Shi Gaomin, the curator of China Grain Museum became Vice-director of China University Museum Professional Committee. Around the same time, 12 universities, including Peking University, Beihang University, Jilin University, Wuhan University, Northwest A&F University, Guangzhou University of Chinese Medicine, Communication University of China, Henan University of Technology, Shaanxi Normal University, Shanghai Jiao Tong University, Tsinghua University and Shanghai University, were awarded with the roles of regional directors and vice-directors of China University Museum Professional Committee.

III. *Chinese Grain History with Illustrations* — the First Historical Book on China's Grain

In the spring of 2016, the national key book of the 12th Five-Year Plan's publishing project — *Chinese Grain History with Illustrations* compiled by Henan University of Technology — was published and distributed. The book has filled a gap in Chinese historiography, and became a best-selling in China's Xinhua Bookstore between 2016 to 2018. It has been unanimously praised by the grain industry and has become an important reference document for China's Grain Culture Science Education Project.

The heart of China is its people. Grain is the basic element of human

为滋养人类生生不息的生命源泉。厚重的粮食情结，造就了博大精深的粮食文化，孕育了栉风沐雨、守望田园的农耕文明，经过漫长岁月的风霜磨砺和蕴涵丰厚的历史积淀，推动人类社会在风雨兼程的前进中异彩纷呈，斑斓辉煌。深邃悠远的粮食发展史，就是一部生动形象的民族生存史，她浸润着灿烂的民族文化乳汁，展示着厚重恢宏的文明精髓，见证着风云激荡的漫长历史，记录着人世间纷繁复杂的沧桑变迁。

鉴此，中国科学院自然科技史权威专家洪光住研究员、中国农业博物馆农业史权威专家曹幸穗教授、粮食文化专家任高堂先生与河南工业大学的专家们一起共同努力，由师高民教授主持统稿，编撰出版了反映粮食史实的科教著作《中国粮食史图说》。《中国粮食史图说》分为科技卷和文化卷两部，科技卷注重研究粮食的起源考证、加工技术等；文化卷则重在揭示粮食与人类及社会发展的关系。文化卷是科技卷的延伸与发展，二者互通互补、相辅相成。以文叙史，以图释义，纵贯古今，放眼南北，以文明的演化衍生为经纬，通过对粮食自然、社会等各种属性的条分缕析，追溯粮食产生发展的渊源轨迹，揭示粮食文化的厚重内涵，诠释粮安天下的普世真谛。

production and life, which is also the primary material resource for social development. Grain has absorbed the essence of heaven and earth, and become the source of life that nourishes human beings like water. A strong food love knot has created a broad and profound grain culture. The farming civilization, often toil outside, cultivating the fields. The brushstrokes of fate have painted a colorful and brilliant frieze of human endeavor. The profound and long history of grain development is vivid history of national survival. It is soaked with the milk of a brilliant national culture. It is a history bursting with the magnificent essence of civilization, which is a testament to humanities flashes of glory and its darkest of nights.

Inspired by such a history researcher Hong Guangzhu, an authoritative expert in the history of natural science and technology of the Chinese Academy of Sciences, and Professor Cao Xingsui, an authoritative expert in the agricultural history from the China Agricultural Museum, and Ren Gaotang, an expert in Grain Culture, worked together with experts from Henan University of Technology to produce the scientific and educational work *Chinese Grain History with Illustrations*, which reflects the historical facts of grain. The draft was presided over by Professor Shi Gaomin. The book is divided into two parts: Science and Technology, Culture. The first volume illustrates the research of the origins of grain and processing technology. The culture volume, focusing on the disclosure of the relationship between the grain and humanbeing as well as the social development, is the extension and development of the science volume. The second volume is the extension and development of the first volume. The two volumes are intertwined and complementary. In the book, history is described with literature, meaning is interpreted with pictures, and the ancient and modern times are looked through, all over the world is looked at, and the evolutionary of civilization is taken as the warp and woof. Through a detail analysis of various attributes of grain, such as nature and society, the book traces the origin and development of grain. The book also reveals the rich culture of grain, and the nature of grain security is explained.

参考文献

[1] 胡凡主编.《简明中国通史》.北京：人民出版社，2012

[2] 吕思勉.《中国通史》.汕头：汕头大学出版社，2014

[3] 斯塔夫里阿诺斯.《全球通史》.北京：北京大学出版社，2012

[4] 中共中央党史研究室.《中国共产党历史》（第二卷：1949－1978）.北京：中共党史出版社，2011

[5] 知行主编.《全球通史》.北京：中国华侨出版社，2013

[6] 亚当·斯密.《国富论》.北京：北京联合出版公司，2014

[7] 石田英一郎等.《人类学》.北京：民族出版社，2008

[8] 梅里尔·温·戴维斯.《人类学》.北京：当代中国出版社，2014

[9] 康拉德·菲利普·科塔克.《人类学》.北京：中国人民大学出版社，2012

[10] 柯美成主编.《理财通鉴——历代食货志全译》.北京：中国财政经济出版社，2007

[11] 中华世纪坛组织委员会编.《中华世纪坛青铜甬道铭文》.北京：中国财政经济出版社，2000

[12] 李建成.《中国粮食文化概说》.北京：中国农业出版社，2011

[13] 张力军、胡泽学主编.《图说中国传统农具》.北京：学苑出版社，2009

References

[1] Hu Fan. *A Brief History of China*. Beijing: People's Publishing House, 2012.

[2] Lu Simian. *General History of China*. Shantou: Shantou University Press, 2014.

[3] Stavrianos, L.S. *A Global History*. Beijing: Peking University Press, 2012.

[4] Party History Research Office of the Central Committee of the Communist Party of China. *History of the Communist Party of China (Volume II: 1949—1978)*. Beijing: CPC History Publishing House, 2011.

[5] Zhi Xing. *A Global History*. Beijing: China Overseas Chinese Publishing House, 2013.

[6] Smith, Adam. *The Wealth of Nations*. Beijing: Beijing United Publishing Co., Ltd., 2014.

[7] Hideichiro Ishida et al. *Anthropology*. Beijing: The Ethnic Publishing House, 2008.

[8] Davies, Merryl Wyn. *Anthropology*. Beijing: Contemporary China Publishing House, 2014.

[9] Kottak, Conrad Phillip. *Anthropology*. Beijing: China Renmin University Press, 2012.

[10] Ke Meicheng. *The Complete Translation of Food and Goods of All Ages*. Beijing: China Financial & Economic Publishing House, 2007.

[11] The China Millennium Monument Committee. *Inscription on Bronze Tunnel of the China Millennium Monument*. Beijing: China Financial & Economic Publishing House, 2000.

[12] Li Jiancheng. *Overview of Chinese Grain Culture*. Beijing: China Agriculture Press, 2011.

[13] Zhang Lijun, Hu Zexue. *Illustrations of Chinese Traditional Agricultural Tools*. Beijing: Xueyuan Publishing House, 2009.

后 记

疫情肆虐，笔耕不断。掩卷深思，感慨良多。

《中华源·河南故事·中原粮谷》在中共河南省委外事工作委员会办公室的直接领导下，在河南工业大学校领导的大力支持下，师高民教授担任中文主编，焦丹院长担任英文主编，多次听取各方专家的指导意见，多方收集资料，几易其稿，历经数月，完成书稿。

在中文编写过程中，与中国科学院自然科学史专家洪光住、粮食文化专家任高堂反复沟通讨论，确定框架内容，中国粮食博物馆藏品部部长谷创业，展陈部部长赵星、李哲以及中国粮食博物馆筹建办的全体老师都参与了资料的收集和图片的拍摄制作。在英文编译过程中，焦丹、张翼、张桂芝、刘希瑞、孙文统、许江梅、赵炜、邰肇丹等老师和同学，以及中央编译局的英国籍译审 Samuel Howarth 先生，付出了大量心血。书能付梓，无不浸透着所有编著者的辛勤汗水。至此，向关心、支持、参与本书编撰的所有领导老师们表示感谢！

现即将付梓出版，恳请国内外读者不吝赐教、批评指正。

师高民
2022.6.16

Postscript

The raging epidemic didn't slow my pen. When I had finished the book, many thoughts poured into my mind.

Under the leadership of the Office of the Foreign Affairs Commission of the CPC Henan Provincial Committee and the suppurt of Henan University of Technology, Professor Shi Gaomin serves as the Chinese editor-in-chief, Jiao Dan serves as the English editor-in-chief. We have listened to many suggestions from a number of grain experts and collected a wide variety of reference. After many drafts and revisions, the completed version has taken shape.

In the process of Chinese compilation, we were in communication with Hong Guangzhu, an expert in the history of natural sciences of the Chinese Academy of Sciences, and Ren Gaotang, an expert in grain culture. They helped us frame the content. Gu Chuangye, director of the Collection Department of the China Grain Museum; Zhao Xing, Li Zhe, directors of Exhibition Department; and all the teachers of Preparatory Office of the China Grain Museum have participated in the collection of materials and the shooting and production of pictures. In the process of English compilation, Jiao Dan, Zhang Yi, Zhang Guizhi, Liu Xirui, Sun Wentong, Xu Jiangmei, Zhao Wei, Tai Zhaodan and other teachers and students, as well as Mr. Samuel Howarth from the Institution for Party History and Literature Research, have made enormous contributions. The book is soaked with the sweat of all the editors. Here, we would like to thank all the leaders and contributors their efforts, who have shown care, support, when assisting with the compilation of this book.

Readers at home and abroad are kindly invited to comment, criticize, and correct the omissions and inaccuracies in the book if they find them.

Shi Gaomin

2022.6.16

附录：中国历史年代简表
Appendix: A Brief Chronology of Chinese History

中国历史年代简表
A Brief Chronology of Chinese History

五帝时代 Period of the Five Legendary Rulers c. 2600 BC–c. 2070 BC	黄帝 Huangdi (Yellow Emperor)	
	颛顼 Zhuanxu	
	帝喾 Diku (Emperor Ku)	
	尧 Yao	
	舜 Shun	
夏 Xia Dynasty	c. 2070 BC–c. 1600 BC	
商 Shang Dynasty	c. 1600 BC–c. 1046 BC	
西周 Western Zhou Dynasty	c. 1046 BC–c. 771 BC	
东周 Eastern Zhou Dynasty 770 BC–256 BC	春秋 Spring and Autumn Period	770 BC–476 BC
	战国 Warring States Period	475 BC–221 BC
秦 Qin Dynasty	221 BC–206 BC	
汉 Han Dynasty 206 BC–220 AD	西汉 Western Han	206 BC–25 AD
	东汉 Eastern Han	25 AD–220 AD
三国 Three Kingdoms 220 AD–280 AD	魏 Wei	220 AD–265 AD
	蜀汉 Shu Han	221 AD–263 AD
	吴 Wu	222 AD–280 AD
晋 Jin Dynasty 265 AD–420 AD	西晋 Western Jin	265 AD–317 AD
	东晋 Eastern Jin	317 AD–420 AD

续表 Continued Table

南北朝 Southern and Northern Dynasties 420 AD-589 AD	南朝 Southern Dynasties	宋 Song	420 AD-479 AD
		齐 Qi	479 AD-502 AD
		梁 Liang	502 AD-557 AD
		陈 Chen	557 AD-589 AD
	北朝 Northern Dynasties	北魏 Northern Wei	386 AD-534 AD
		东魏 Eastern Wei	534 AD-550 AD
		北齐 Northern Qi	550 AD-577 AD
		西魏 Western Wei	535 AD-556 AD
		北周 Northern Zhou	557 AD-581 AD
隋 Sui Dynasty			581 AD-618 AD
唐 Tang Dynasty			618 AD-907 AD
五代十国 Five Dynasties and Ten States	五代 Five Dynasties 907 AD-960 AD	后梁 Later Liang	907 AD-923 AD
		后唐 Later Tang	923 AD-936 AD
		后晋 Later Jin	936 AD-947 AD
		后汉 Later Han	947 AD-950 AD
		后周 Later Zhou	951 AD-960 AD
	十国 Ten States 902 AD-979 AD	北汉 Northern Han	951 AD-979 AD
		吴 Wu	902 AD-937 AD
		吴越 Wuyue	907 AD-978 AD
		闽 Min	909 AD-945 AD
		南汉 Southern Han	917 AD-971 AD
		荆南(又称"南平") Jingnan (Nanping)	924 AD-963 AD
		楚 Chu	927 AD-951 AD
		南唐 Southern Tang	937 AD-975 AD
		前蜀 Former Shu	907 AD-925 AD
		后蜀 Later Shu	934 AD-965 AD

续表 Continued Table

宋 Song Dynasty 960 AD-1279 AD	北宋 Northern Song	960 AD-1127 AD
	南宋 Southern Song	1127 AD-1279 AD
辽 Liao (契丹 Qidan/Khitan)	907 AD-1125 AD	
西夏 Xixia (Tangut)	1038 AD-1227 AD	
金 Jin	1115 AD-1234 AD	
元 Yuan Dynasty	1206 AD-1368 AD	
明 Ming Dynasty	1368 AD-1644 AD	
清 Qing Dynasty	1616 AD-1911 AD	
中华民国 Republic of China	1912 AD-1949 AD	
中华人民共和国 People's Republic of China	1949 AD-	